Michael Sykes joined the Royal Navy from Sheffield as a boy and later joined Submarines. He left in 1987 as a Lt. Commander and after directorships in both public and private sectors, he went to Croatia then Slovenia with his wife, Cathy, and opened a language school and translation agency for 15 years as well as examining for Cambridge University. From 2010, he Chaired a large Anti-Piracy company and travelled extensively on business through Europe and Asia.

He has spoken at conferences about privatisation, English, and piracy, been interviewed by the BBC, and written articles for papers and journals. His home is in Hampshire.

Dedication

To my wife, Cathy, with immense thanks for her tolerance, support and encouragement.

Michael Sykes

WHY THE WORLD IS SPEAKING ENGLISH – A SIDEWAYS LOOK

AUSTIN MACAULEY PUBLISHERS™

LONDON • CAMBRIDGE • NEW YORK • SHARJAH

A CIP catalogue record for this title is available from the British Library.

ISBN 9781788237369 (Paperback)
ISBN 9781788237376 (Hardback)
ISBN 9781788237383 (E-Book)
www.austinmacauley.com

First Published (2017)
Austin Macauley Publishers Ltd™
25 Canada Square
Canary Wharf
London
E14 5LQ

Acknowledgements

Thanks to my good friend Phil Rich for his casual but brilliant suggestion.

Table of Contents

What's It All About?

English, as we know it today, was created about 900 years ago to solve a bit of a communication problem in the relatively small, insignificant, north European island of England. This language, created by a small island population, has since grown disproportionately and propelled itself around the globe to become a major contributor to world communications. It has even been launched into the outer reaches of deep space to tell possible inhabitants of other stars and galaxies about the human race.

Because of that very powerful motive behind most creation, necessity, English is a very simple language in its structure and grammar, and therefore, simple to learn. Its simplicity, adaptability, history, the British Empire, the American dream, Disney and Hollywood, Silicon Valley, and even T-shirts, have all contributed to its growth momentum, which seems to be accelerating in the 21st century.

This short book is a slightly whimsical 'Sideways Look' at how English has increasingly become the principal international world language in a rapidly changing, and increasingly globalised, world. It considers the merits of this growth and speculates if it will continue.

11

It looks at the role of English in the remarkable and unstoppable communications, and travel revolution that is happening right now.

Although controversial at times, this book contains facts, opinion, speculation, some humour, and is, I hope, relaxed reading. It is aimed at anybody interested in the phenomena of the English language. It is not an academic book but explains why English is simple, practical, flexible and adaptable, with considerable advantages over other languages, enabling it to have such significant success. It looks at the history of English and explains how it was 'created' remarkably quickly as a practical solution to a communication problem between two very different people, and explains why it has spread so successfully to become the world's most widely used language.

It deals with the advantages of sharing language, and disadvantages of not sharing. The thorny issues of links between language and cultural identity, and language politics are examined. The very high costs of using different languages in countries and in organisations such as the EU are examined, as well as comparing British English and American English. It reflects on some English language peculiarities. It looks at the differences in unity within the populations of the USA, the EU, and the old USSR, and the language implications. It looks at the consequences for the English language in the ever increasing globalisation.

Biblical legend relates that humans once spoke one language, and were then cursed with separate 'tongues' as a punishment. However, we now live in such an extraordinary, fast moving and critical time in world history and evolution, with increasing interdependence between nations, that world-wide communication may once again be a powerful driver for a common world language.

1. It's Good to Talk: The Human Gift

When the people of Babel built a tower to reach heaven,
He viewed this as disrespectful and confounded their
speech so they could no longer understand each other
and scattered them around the world.
(Genesis)

Would the world be a better place if its people all spoke the same language and were able to better understand each other? Are we beginning to overcome the 'punishment' of using different languages that the book of 'Genesis' in the Bible tells us were imposed upon humankind, and do we increasingly want to communicate more easily and readily between the different peoples of the world to increase understanding? It would be a remarkable achievement if this did happen.

As humans we have this wonderful gift called language. But, it is not easy to define what constitutes an individual language and to count the numbers that exist. It is often difficult to differentiate between a macro-language, a language, and a language-dialect. For instance, China can be counted as one language, or a macro-language, or many different regional languages.

Equally, estimating the numbers that speak a language can be very difficult, if not nearly impossible in some cases. One only has to think of the vast rain-forests of South America containing many different tribes to realise the difficulties. Estimation of numbers of speaking a language can be obscured by a lack of central administration and records, and can even be distorted by the politics of a nation's language that demand separate recognition to their close neighbour's language, even though the two languages may be almost identical in many ways (Serbian and Croatian are examples in Europe).

There are around 7000 languages in the world, though different estimates do exist. This seems a lot, but you have to examine the distribution of population to languages more closely. In fact, 85% of the world's population (of 7.3 billion) are covered by about 100 languages. Around 25 languages have 50 million or more speakers, and cover 61% of the world population. As well as the major European languages, these 25 languages include Chinese, Arabic, Hindi, Bengali, Russian, Japanese, Korean, Turkish, Urdu, Persian, and others. A further 45 languages then include populations of less than 50 million but more than 15 million, and include languages like Polish, Burmese, Ukrainian, Dutch, Serbian, Somali, and many more. Below this there is a long taper of decreasing numbers speaking different languages, and most languages are used only by a relatively small number of people. The world's most diverse language region is Papua New Guinea where over 800 different languages are used, but this is highly unusual. Many languages of the world have similarities, though many are very different.

All languages, though, have one purpose; to enable people, tribes, communities, societies and nations to communicate between themselves. Most of us take language for granted, most of the time. It is just something we use and have used since we can remember. But, our ability to use language is incredibly important and distinguishes us from all other animal species with which we share our planet. We humans are comparatively frail in physique and stamina, so how on earth have we managed to become such a 'master animal' on this planet, and developed well beyond all other species in dominance and sophistication? What has enabled this?

The short answer is our brain size, which has grown through evolution, giving us greater intelligence than other animals. One way in which we have used this intelligence is to invent language (besides trying to destroy each other fairly regularly). Using language enables us to work together in groups, tribes and communities and, more importantly, 'plan' in ways that other animals are unable to do. It is this ability to plan and co-ordinate that has enabled humans to outwit predators and hostile climates, and survive; and having survived, devise ways to master the environment and protect ourselves whilst developing further.

Language allows us to communicate ideas between each other, and explain things in detail. We can describe threats, dangers, ideas, and opportunities to fellow humans. It allows us to negotiate with partners, within families, with rivals, and within our wider communities. Negotiation is trying to reach agreement by discussion and is far more widely used, by everybody, than people realise. In fact, it is constantly used. When we try to agree with our partner whether to stay in or go to the movies, we are negotiating. Getting our children to do something we want is often through negotiation. We constantly negotiate our way through life, in the home, at work, in our community, though we don't think of it as negotiation. It is a vital human attribute; and language is the critical skill needed.

The use of language has gradually broadened over the centuries. Originally, language was used 'internally', within tribes and small communities, as this was all that was necessary. People lived in relatively small communities and either did not travel, or travelled in small groups, usually avoiding other groups. So, the language of groups would normally be exclusive to that group. Basic negotiation would still have been normal within these groups, but language was used almost exclusively for internal communication, and not for communicating with the outside world.

Throughout most of the world these groups gradually enlarged, or merged, with other groups for various reasons, and the strongest languages started to dominate and expand. Languages were still mainly used internally, but sometimes language would be used to negotiate 'externally' with other groups, and this would have been difficult because of language barriers. This enlargement of tribal or community groups continued, and eventually 'nations' started to emerge, usually speaking the same language, maybe with strong regional dialects, and many smaller languages were gradually condensed into national languages. Some of these national languages expanded further – by colonial expansion, for example – and some contracted, often because of conquest. But, except for trade and diplomatic negotiations, language remained, for the most part, an internal form of communication.

This has changed significantly in recent centuries as language is needed more and more for external use, usually for work, trade, business, and travel, but also to increasingly understand world news and issues. This increase in external communication has accelerated significantly since the early 1990s with the astounding revolution in communication capability, by the phone and internet for instance, and easier air travel. Internal communication within groups and nations still dominates day to day life, but the growth in external communications outside a language group has increased dramatically.

Although English is just one of the world's 7000 languages, for some reason, or reasons, English has relentlessly spread around the world for the past few centuries, and in recent decades its use around the world has accelerated. Why is this? Why has English been adopted so widely, and not another language? What's so special about English? It seems to be taken for granted that English is the international language of choice, but there are a lot of competitor languages out there.

My opening question of 'Would the world be a better place if we all spoke the same language and be better able to understand each other' may well be starting to happen already, anyway, by the use of English. Is this a good thing? And why is it English?

This short book takes a 'sideways look' at the use and creation of language in general, and English in particular. It looks at the almost accidental invention of English and its early history, its appeal, importance, spread, and its ever-increasing role in the world to support the communication's revolution that is also happening, now. It raises issues about national identity and culture, the politics of language, the cost of language, the controversial issue of globalisation, and the benefits of universal communication. Thorny issues will also be raised, such as comparisons between the English speaking USA and the multi-lingual European Union. It will say some things that may be obvious to some and well known, things you agree with, things that are not obvious, some new facts, and some things with which you may strongly disagree. Above all, I hope it will stimulate your interest concerning this fascinating phenomena of why the world is speaking English.

A parallel communication revolution to this growth in English is happening now, in the time we live. So, first let's look at this communication revolution, and how it is interacting with one of the greatest accidental gifts to the world; the English language.

2. The Modern Communication Revolution

We are living through a communication revolution which is one of the most important advances in modern history. Yet, we hardly notice it now, or we just take it for granted, probably because it is happening everywhere, seems to affect everybody, and is generally helpful, positive, and welcomed. We have probably become immune to the communication revolution that is so obvious.

There are two parts to this revolution. One part of this communication revolution is the means by which we can communicate and meet other inhabitants of the globe, electronically and by travel, and this has accelerated startlingly fast since about the year 2000; whilst the other part of the revolution, the growth in the use of English, has been gradually happening for many decades.

Both revolutions are developing together, at different speeds, and are not knowingly linked, but do affect each other. In future years this means of communication revolution will be recognised by historians as being as important as the 19th century industrial revolution, affecting many different people, of all types, world-wide, and people of all ages.

Let us look at the first part of this revolution, the means to communicate, mainly due to advances in digital communication. This is creating communication opportunities and the need, or desire, for people to communicate across wide distances around the world, either verbally, or by electronic media, or by increasingly efficient air travel. Within about 15 years we have progressed from very expensive international phone calls for the few, or letter writing via the postage system, to instant and affordable world-wide communications available to masses of people. Instead of expensive land-line phone calls overseas (can anyone remember those?) most people can now communicate with anybody, to anywhere in the world, instantly, via mobile cell phones, cheaply; or using the internet, or other electronic 'platforms', almost for free.

The speed of this communication revolution has been breath-taking, and it is amazing how quickly we have become used to something so new and revolutionary, and we forget just how dramatically things have changed. The figures below illustrate the pace of change in global communications by looking at the use of mobile (cell) phones and the internet (m=million):

	1990	**2010**	**2016**
Cell phone users:	12m	4000m	5500m (about)
Internet users:	2m	1800m	3600m
World population:			7300m

These figures are astonishing. It was about the turn of the millennium, 2000, that the explosion in global communications started to accelerate, becoming available to masses of people and not just a few. Taking the figures above, in 2016 a staggering 75% of the world had access to cell-phones and almost 50% had internet access. This really is revolutionary.

World behaviour statistics are notoriously difficult to accurately determine, but production figures are less difficult. It is known with more certainty that in 2015 the total number of mobile phones in use throughout the world was over seven billion. The world's population is about 7.3 billion, so in theory 7 billion phones is equivalent to 95% of the world's population. Of course this does not mean that everyone has a mobile phone. Many users have more than one mobile phone, and in places like North Korea the user percentage is thought to be as low as 8%. However accurate or not these total figures really are, there is no doubt that communications around the world has experienced a tremendous revolution in the past two decades, and it is still happening.

Global communication also means travel. The growth in the last few decades of cheaper, more efficient, and safer air travel has also been revolutionary. The general public from many countries are now travelling the world to explore and discover places that once only the rich or privileged could dream of visiting. Only 60 years ago, in the UK, we essentially had London, Heathrow for air travel, and old newsreels show the propeller driven planes being boarded by passengers, carrying their bags, and walking from the existing terminal to board their planes. Now Heathrow has five very large terminals and is one of the busiest airports in the world. Dubai, 60 years ago, was a desert. Now it has the world's largest airport. When I was a child, people looked up to the skies when they saw or heard an aeroplane, as it was still unusual. Now, if you glance upwards most times of the day you can spot several aircraft crossing our skies. That is how much air travel has increased.

How does our multi-lingual world cope with this explosion in global communications and travel? Even today, many people just communicate across their own country, within their own region and within their own language group. However, many want, or need, or must, increasingly communicate outside their own country and language zone.

This is where the second part of the revolution comes in, which is the phenomenal growth in the use of English language in past decades, and the role it is playing in this astonishing communication revolution. We need to look at this phenomenal growth in English and try to find out why it has happened, and the implications.

3. Restless, Ever-Changing English

If you are an everyday user of the English language as your native tongue, you probably rarely think about its significance, effects, history, controversies, or growth. Why should you? It is just something you use naturally? Unless English language is your trade as an English teacher, English writer, linguistics specialist, or (horror of horrors) a grammarian, there is no reason for you to think about it very often. It's just 'there'; used by you and taken for granted.

Why should you think about the language you constantly and easily use? Mostly we communicate with family, colleagues, acquaintances, and the immediate world around us, without thinking about what we are using, or how we use it. The days of being corrected for our grammar belong to our youth and past school days – if we were corrected at all, that is. And anyway, who cares about that sort of thing anymore? Because of texting, tweeting, social media, and the increasingly cosmopolitan societies we live in, we are constantly adjusting English grammar and spelling 'rules', often without realising it. Even the Queen of England has changed her use of English. You only have to listen to her broadcasts 60 years ago compared with today to hear how much her English has changed. Her voice used to sound like cut glass, with crisp articulation and, by today's standards, sounded abrupt and quiet cold. Her tone, delivery and even vocabulary has changed to be concomitant with modern times, and that is normal, natural and to be welcomed. English is changing under our very noses, but a lot of the time we don't think about it.

Possibly we only think about our English when doing word quizzes, such as crosswords, or trying to find the best word to express a feeling or describe something, especially when writing. You might occasionally be thankful for your English as it is enables you to watch Hollywood movies without using those tiresome sub-titles; and when travelling abroad you can usually find someone who understands English; and in airports and such places English is invariably used for public notices alongside the local language, which is very useful for us English speakers (or, is it 'we English speakers'). Otherwise, we just accept our language. Why shouldn't we?

Perhaps occasionally we struggle a little when listening to very pronounced English accents, or non-English speakers using our language? We probably, occasionally, make judgements about people through their use of English when they are using good, or not so good, grammar and vocabulary. And perhaps when we listen to someone speaking we sometimes sigh inwardly, or chuckle about their misuse, or different use, of our language. Or, alternatively, we may be impressed by someone's English, or even feel a mite intimidated; or, conversely, struggle to understand what someone is saying, finding their dialect or accent difficult to interpret.

Does it really matter? A famous English author of the early 20th century, George Bernard Shaw, thought so and wrote in 'Preface to Pygmalion' (My Fair Lady):

"It is impossible for an Englishman to open his mouth without making some other Englishman hate or despise him."

What he meant is that spoken English, in his day, invariably signified the speaker's 'class', be it higher or lower, and consequently a listener could despise the speaker's class and upbringing, and their use of language. Perhaps such class judgements based on speech, or based on anything, are outdated now in this increasingly classless 21st century?

What is certain, is that there are now many forms of spoken English. There is certainly not one 'standard' English language anymore, and sometimes the English we hear does not sound like the language we normally use as our own. Have we not all had those very challenging experiences on the telephone with those linguistic nightmares called 'call centres'?

In Britain, despite our denials, I believe many people still classify other people by how they speak our language, albeit sub-consciously. We place them into the country or region of their origin, possibly their level of education, possibly their occupation, perhaps even their social 'class'. We might not think so, or admit it, but I suspect we do sub-consciously. I don't think we 'despise' different users as much as in Bernard Shaw's day, though perhaps some people still do – and perhaps many of us do, but deny it? Undeniably, alongside the way people dress, spoken language can help us make rapid assessments about people, even if this assessment is not accurate.

Possibly we give our English more thought when writing rather than when speaking? Perhaps we sometimes hesitate, consider the best word to use, or whether we should say something this way, or that way? Maybe we hesitate and have to think about writing 'its' or 'it's'? Do we use 'either' or 'neither', with 'or' or 'nor'? And when do we use 'I were' instead of 'I was'? Is it really important in this modern age, except to a few, usually older, fuddy-duddies that like to get upset about what they consider is the incorrect use of English?

We might be enraged by telephone operatives that seem to speak a form of English that is often almost unintelligible and, following such experiences, we permit ourselves a quiet, or not so quiet rant about having to deal with such barely intelligible English (hastily making sure we make it clear that we have "absolutely nothing at all" against people of different ethnicity, but why can't people who speak proper English answer the phone, dammit). Although I'm embarrassed to admit it, I know I have – haven't you?

However, most people, most of the time, have neither the inclination nor time to wonder about the English language's idiosyncrasies, complexities, variations, evolution, or peculiarities; or wonder about its seemingly relentless spread around the world. Even less do we think about its origins, controversies, and even strong emotions that our language can provoke.

Well, if you are an everyday user of English, normally uninterested in linguistics (or is it disinterested?), then you are the very type of person at which I aim this short book. It is definitely not aimed at linguistic specialists, grammar geeks, academics, or anyone searching for deep explanations of spelling, correct language usage, grammar or syntax; and does not attempt to be an academic analysis of our language. This is a relatively brief, sometimes slightly tongue-in-cheek explanation, of where our language originates, and why its origin is actually important. It explains how English has evolved, how it is regulated, how many people really use English, some of the major controversies in its use, how using the same language can save considerable costs, it describes its remorseless, restless, global spread, and how English is acting as an agent for change. Its possible future will also be considered.

How would the world manage without this growing international language? Could a similar major language take its place, such as Spanish, or French, or Chinese? Why is English the national language in the USA, for instance, where many other languages were used much more widely than English by the original settlers of that vast continent, well before English speakers arrived?

Who knows what drives English? There is no doubt that English has had, and is still having, a profound effect on the world and continues to spread restlessly and relentlessly, and it may have an even greater effect upon the world in the future.

4. Where Did English Come from, and Why?

So where does the English language come from? It didn't just 'happen', or appear from nowhere. It had to have its origins somewhere, somehow.

The obvious answer is it originated in England, but that is hardly a comprehensive or helpful answer, considering the Anglo Saxon majority population of 'England' spoke a form of German, and the Viking minority population, mainly in the north of England, a type of Norse. And then, the new arrivals to England, the Norman conquerors, spoke Old French. In addition, the normal 'recorders' of our island's activities used Latin or French for records, and the dwindling number of the original inhabitants of England, who had been remorselessly driven westwards and northwards into Wales, Scotland, and Cornwall, by the different invaders, spoke forms of the Celtic tongue. None of these languages – of the Anglo-Saxons, Vikings, or Celts – would be vaguely recognisable today by your average speaker of English.

So, how was English created in this Saxon, Norse, Celtic, French speaking melting pot of England? Why was it created and how was it created when the old Anglo

Saxon language easily dominated amongst the island inhabitants and then, later, England was under the iron domination of the new French speaking Normans? Either Anglo Saxon or French could have won the language competition, but neither did. When and why was English created? Is there something special about it?

The answer is very interesting and, I think, an intriguing mystery of 'language creation' that explains a lot about the spread of English. This English language of Shakespeare, Wordsworth, Dickens, Austen, Lincoln, Churchill, Scott-Fitzgerald, Kennedy, Bob Dylan... which now belongs to many nations and is used in different forms all over the world, was created extraordinarily quickly by two, barely communicating groups of practical, though very opposed, people. One group was the majority, indigenous residents of England, the Anglo-Saxons, and the other group were the new boys on the block, the new resident cum conquerors, the Normans. These two groups certainly had no liking of each other, in fact positively disliked each other very much, but they also realised that they had to communicate, somehow, and create a mutual 'working' language and live together.

And, that is why English was created – because it had to be created. It was all a bit of an invention through necessity. And, necessity is invariably a very devious mother of invention. What follows is my explanation of why, when, and how English was invented. However, before we look at English in detail, let's first look at language creation in general.

5. Creating a Language

Languages, in reality, are not normally 'invented' by people huddled together deliberately creating a new language. There is one exception, Esperanto, which was the very unsuccessful, artificially created 'world language', devised in the late 19th century, and which never gained popularity anywhere, and virtually disappeared from view in the 20th and 21st century.

Sustainable and accepted working languages, big and small, are created by evolution, probably over long periods of time. However, the idea of deliberately creating a new language, like English, is a provocative and interesting thought; and an idea we will return to.

The world's languages have evolved. Although we will never know for certain how they evolved, they probably started with grunts and other sounds that gradually became standardised within a family, or small group, or tribe, so that members could basically communicate with each other, invariably at the most basic level of transactional communication for everyday living and survival; to hunt, to eat, to work together, to mate, to warn of danger, to agree and disagree, and to protect themselves.

I imagine, in those swirling pre-historical mists of time, people would want to have sounds that could be quickly and clearly recognised by other group members for indicating communication wishes such as: yes, no, it's mine, that there, this here, I'm hungry, I need food, we need water, let's go, stop, be quiet, come near me, this is mine, 'do you want' type questions, and so on. Such a limited number of key sounds would gradually be standardised amongst a group, and expanded and elaborated over time.

We cannot assume they would have used the range of speech noises we use today. Positioning the tongue in the mouth, using our lips in different positions, and expelling or inhaling air through the mouth in different ways to form a wide range of sounds as quickly as we do, would not come naturally. People have to learn how to use their lips, tongue, cheeks, breathing, and to develop tiny mouth and throat muscles to produce different sounds. Learning how to articulate language is not unlike having to learn how to use a musical instrument. It needs time and lots of practice.

For instance, English speakers easily make the sound 'th', as in 'thin', by placing the tongue to the roof of the mouth against the top teeth and pushing air out past the tongue between slightly open lips. We do this very quickly, without thought, but we had to learn how to do it. Many non-English speakers find this 'th' sound very difficult and unnatural. Why? Because native-English-speakers have been taught how to create the 'th' sound from infancy, mostly by copying their parents, whereas non-native-English-speakers have not.

Conversely, English speakers find many of the guttural, back-of-the-throat sounds used in many languages such as German, Dutch, Nordic and Arabic, very difficult to reproduce. Again, it is because we have not been trained to use such sounds, and have not developed the necessary tiny mouth and throat muscles.

It is probable that the human mouth, jaw, voice-box, and tongue have evolved to allow the maximum articulation of a wide range of sounds. This physical evolution probably took a very long time, maybe hundreds or even thousands of years. We cannot know for certain as we don't have records.

If we believe a language gradually evolves, how fast is 'gradual'? The nearest we come to observing a language-learning process is observing babies learning how to speak. If you have seen this process with babies, think how fast language is absorbed and used by them. It might seem slow to parents but, in fact, babies learn incredibly fast. Parents might wish for the day when baby can understand them and use sentences though, in reality, within quite a short time a toddler is beginning to be intelligible and use relatively sophisticated language to convey meaning and facts, preferences, and emotions. They learn by observation, sound, and mimicry. This demonstrates that humans can learn very quickly though, of course, we must bear in mind that babies are learning a language that has already been created. How long that language originally took to formulate, we can only guess.

No other animal on this planet has our ability to learn how to communicate and use very sophisticated language very quickly with other members of a community. We can learn much, and very fast, when we have to. Perhaps that ever watchful mother of invention, necessity, means that languages were more quickly 'invented' than we imagine – who knows? The use of language probably evolved hand in hand (or tongue in cheek) with our brain sizes over a long period of time, but we will never be certain.

Why are there such a wide variety of languages? Again, we can't know for certain, but it may be that the specific sounds of one language were created by a dominant member, or the cleverest member, of a group or tribe, and this was then copied by the other members. So, the words of the language come down to what sound that person originally decided would mean 'let's go', for instance. We do know, through linguistic studies, that certain words seem to 'travel' and appear in neighbouring languages, although they might slightly change. Many European languages share many similar words even though, when language was being invented thousands of years ago, travel was very difficult. Some words have 'travelled' a long way it seems. A good and easy example of a word that seemed to travel well is 'no', which in different European languages is no, non, nej, nay, njet, ne, nien ... all very similar.

Though we will never know the answer about how language was created or travelled, as there are no sound recordings of ancient history, intuitively we can assume the subsequent spread of a language after it had been created would depend upon the type of environment in which it existed. The spread of each language had constraints of landscape and travel, safety, weather, how many people were in the tribe, how much contact was made with other groups of humans, if any; and whether the group or tribe were forced to travel and trade with other tribes to survive.

We know that some tribes had much more favourable physical environments for spreading their language and possibly this is one reason why some languages seem to have spread over a wide area (but, there are many other factors), whilst other languages are confined to quite a small area, such as within mountainous areas, or on islands.

This speed of language spread and its acceptance becomes important when we start to speculate on the use and spread of modern English since it first appeared, 900 years ago. When English became the language resembling what we recognise today, it seemed to spread quickly throughout England. That was because England had relatively easy physical travel and communication, with roads and many tracks, networks of villages and towns, and no large mountain ranges, or deserts to obstruct progress. In addition, England already had in existence, even 900 years ago, villages and towns with their own congregations, markets, travelling tinkers, and even the written word (for a privileged few), and sometimes public notices (though very few would be able to read). England would have been a comparatively easy environment for the spread of a 'new' language.

I say 'comparatively easy environment'. It is true that travel throughout Britain 900 years ago was not easy in comparison with modern times, and was usually by foot. However, travel throughout Britain was possible, and did happen, with no daunting obstacles to prevent it. So, compared with ancient times, when most main languages were being formed, the new English language, when it 'arrived', as will be explained shortly, could be spread around the country relatively easily, within quite a short time.

When considering the spread of a language, in addition to physical travel and contact, there is also the powerful factor of motivation; the motivation to have a common language by which to communicate. Quite possibly some tribes in ancient times did not want to communicate with other tribes. There may have been open hostility between some neighbouring tribes and, even if not hostility, perhaps there was no perceived need to communicate, so motivation to try and communicate externally with others would be low. Presumably this is why the tribes of Papua New Guinea have so many different languages, as they didn't feel the need to mix, or dominate.

But it is almost certain that within Britain, the need and motivation to communicate across the land would have been quite high, because of the exchange of goods and family connections. Contact between the indigenous people of England was well established. They had places to discuss news, exchange ideas, and matters of mutual interest. They recognised between themselves that some sort of feudal or tribal bond existed, even if the concept of being one nation, England, was not yet established.

Because the written form of a language always arrives much later than the spoken language, it is impossible that we can ever know how spoken language was created, or evolved, as none of the language inventors could record doing it. We can only guess how a language happened, how it was created, and how it spread. And that is true for most of the world's languages. Except for English.

English is quite different and is a remarkable exception to this general ignorance of knowing when languages began and how they were created. We do know when English, as a recognisable language, started to exist and from where it came. We also know that it spread remarkably quickly once it appeared. We know this because the Saxons were relatively good at keeping written records (in Anglo-Saxon) for about 300 years, and so were the Normans (in French) that took over running England from the Saxons. So, the approximate dates and stages of the appearance of English can be quite well identified. That is a very interesting aspect of English that is not available to most other languages.

How, rather than when, English was created is another question completely. So, let's now take a closer look at this invention of English.

6. 1066 AD, and All That

Let us go back in time to just before that very famous year in England's history, 1066 AD – when new Norman masters conquered England. Up to that fateful year, most written work for government, law, and religion was in Latin, as favoured by the clergy and the learned elite. Increasingly some written work was in Anglo-Saxon. King Alfred, an Anglo Saxon king, had created the Anglo-Saxon Chronicles in the 9th century and, under his instructions, they were written in Anglo-Saxon rather than Latin.

The main form of spoken communication in England for most of the population was this language which we will refer to as Anglo-Saxon which, in practice was a mixture of different Germanic-type languages and dialects, with some Norse (Viking) influence especially in the north of England, previously the lands of the Danelaw (effectively under the control of the Vikings, or Danes).

Before 1066, these islands were mainly populated by people that had originally come to England from mainland Europe, from the regions that we describe today as Germany, Denmark, Holland, Norway, and Sweden, though these regions did not exist then as nation states. This migration into England had been during the great period of mass migration all across Europe, during the so-called *Volkerwanderung* (folks are wandering), otherwise known as the Barbarian Invasions. When these tribes of Angles, Saxons, Jutes, and later Vikings arrived on English shores from these continental regions, they displaced the existing Celtic speaking population, sometimes called ancient Britons or Romano-Britons, and replaced their Celtic language with their own north European Germanic-Nordic languages. Remnants of the old Celtic language can be found in today in the north and west of Britain, in Wales, some Scottish islands, and even Cornwall.

But in the bulk of the island that is now called England, the languages of the new Germanic Saxon and Norse invaders displaced the Celtic language. Then, gradually, these different but similar Germanic tribal languages fused together into a language that can broadly be called Anglo-Saxon. This was happening, incrementally, from the time the Romans left England (or Britannica as it was then known) in the early AD 400s, until the 800–900s when England was emerging from being a Heptarchy (seven kingdoms) to being an identifiable single nation. So, the evolution and establishment of the Anglo Saxon language from all its donor languages probably took about 400–500 years.

In numbers, the main bulk of the new settlers were from what is known today as Denmark, Jutland and north Netherlands, especially from the part now known as Frisia (they even brought their own black and white cows). It is said that the sound of the spoken language of modern Frisia bears an eerie resemblance to modern English.

Many words of England's 'Anglo-Saxon' language were not so very different from today's modern

German/Nordic languages. The words used would have differed between areas of England, and even differed in how the same words were actually pronounced, depending on the origin of the settlers. The spoken language was not standardised, but people from different parts of England, and therefore from different tribes, would have been comprehensible to each other with some effort and not too much difficulty. Words used would have included sounds such as:

fater (father) mutter (mother) bruder (brother) sie (she) mann (man)

kuh (cow) laam (lamb) goes (goose) schwein (swine) miel (meal) buter (butter)

foda (food) k'niv (knife) bier (beer) hest (horse)

haar (hair) verk (work) hart (hard) hand (hand) buch (book) liebe (love) sex (sex)

toalet (toilet) snie (snow) froast (frost) blau (blue) trije (three) fjour (four)

Many of these printed words are recognisable today in their modern English form (shown in brackets), though much of their old pronunciation would sound very different to the ears of modern English speakers as the vowels had different sounds. For instance, mutter (mother), would have had a deep 'u' and more rolling 'r', and been pronounced something more like 'mooterr'.

Sentence grammar, word order, and word sounds of the Anglo-Saxon language would have been very different. Nouns – things – like the nouns listed above, would be categorised as either male, female, or neuter, with different word endings depending on their use (this changing of word endings depending upon its use is known as 'inflection'). For instance fot (foot), which is a 'male' word, could be fot, fet, fotes, fota, fote, or fotum depending upon how it was used in a sentence.

Each noun would also use different 'articles' ('a' and 'the' are modern English articles) depending if they were male, female, plural, possessive, object, subject, etc. For instance, in modern English we have one definite article, 'the'. In Anglo Saxon 'the' could be: se, thaet, seo, tha, thone, thaes, thaera, thara, tham, thon, thy; depending upon the word. Pretty complicated stuff!

We could, today, recognise some Anglo Saxon vocabulary described above, but the grammar and sentence construction was very different and would be incomprehensible to the modern English speaker. So, it is not unreasonable to say that the majority language of England, pre 1066, was old Germanic-Norse we are conveniently calling Anglo-Saxon (and, confusingly, sometimes called 'Old English'). This Anglo Saxon 'English' was very unlike the English we know today.

Then, in 1066, this Anglo-Saxon island (Angle-land became England) changed dramatically, and forever. The French speaking Normans under William, Duke of Normandy, successfully invaded and occupied this island. After killing the unfortunate and unlucky King Harold II and defeating his Anglo Saxon army, they then did what most invaders do for a few rock n' roll years; they beat, pillaged, destroyed, subdued, raped and ravaged the existing population; creating mayhem and a very crushed, sullen population of Anglo-Saxons, with their new Norman overlords in charge. These Norman overlords lurked in their ubiquitous forts and castles, with superior organisation and better weapons and armour, but Saxons were still, by far, very much the majority of the island's population and still speaking their Anglo-Saxon language.

However, unlike many invaders in other countries, the Normans were not going to return to their homeland, and they fully intended to stay. And stay they did. This was no quick 'get in and get out' operation. The Anglo-Saxon lands were divided between the conquering Norman Lords loyal to William the Conqueror – also known as William the Norman, William Duke of Normandy, and to some William the Bastard (though probably not to his face). And gradually the new Norman Lords stopped their destruction and pillaging, and many brought to England their own Norman families, or imported Norman or French wives. The Saxon's finally realised that their new Norman overlords were here to stay and, despite the best efforts of some local heroes, like Hereward and Robin Hood, there was really very little they could do about it.

Gradually, but with increasing importance, it was realised that the two communities had to start communicating as their inter-dependency increased. They could not co-exist as two separate communities forever, and they had to deal with each other on major issues and day-to-day matters. They had to learn to communicate to better understand each other. But how, with such different languages?

The Normans (originally Norse men, northern man, that had invaded and settled in northern France 200 years previously – hence the name Nor'man) spoke a form of French which they had assimilated from their newly acquired French homeland, now called Normandy. Their Norman-French vocabulary had some words similar to the Old Saxon language because the French language did share its roots with its previous conquerors, the Germanic 'Franks'.

Like the Anglo Saxon language, Norman French also had male and female for their nouns (le and la). And, like the Anglo-Saxons, their verb endings changed significantly depending if the verb was used for I, you, we, he, she, them.

Most of the necessary communication between the conquered Anglo-Saxon population and their new Norman conquerors was, in the early days, between and within the lower orders of society; between workers, tradesmen, soldiers, even lovers; for day-to-day events, orders, requests, purchases, and dealings. The Norman Lords would spend most of their time, in the first few decades, dealing with each other in their own Norman-French language and not mixing with those awfully common Saxon peasants with their terribly harsh sounding, vulgar language. Nonetheless, life between common Normans and Saxons had to go on, in the market places of towns and villages, and in the Courts of Justice ...

So, the two communities increasingly had to learn to communicate, somehow. The two communities had to integrate by necessity. Unlike the previous conquerors of this island – the Romans – the Normans did not see themselves as temporary resident-suppressors who did their time here, kept themselves to themselves, and then returned home, and did not need to have meaningful communication with the natives. The Normans were here to stay, permanently, and they knew it. End game. This was their new home and, therefore, they had to integrate and live with, and communicate with, the indigenous Saxons, who were the majority of the population.

So, a language of mutual communication had to be found. Either the Normans had to learn Anglo-Saxon, or the Saxons had to learn Norman-French. Or, a new compromise language had to be created that both sides could understand.

Should the Normans learn Anglo-Saxon; or the Anglo-Saxons learn French? Wouldn't that be an obvious solution? Many invaders of countries either imposed their own language, or were absorbed into the local language. For instance, the Normans that had invaded northern France had ended up speaking French. Centuries later, the conquering Spanish always compelled their conquered natives to speak Spanish. However, here in this island, there were two very stubborn people; the dominant Normans and the sullen, but majority, Anglo-Saxons. Neither side would give way on this question of which language to use.

The Normans probably saw the Saxons as inferior people, with a harsh sounding, guttural language that was also pretty complicated, though the Saxons had the benefit of sheer population numbers and indigenous residency.

In addition, it is not easy for adults to learn a new, very different foreign language, as the Saxon language was quite different to the Norman language. Gradually, but inescapably, it was realised a compromise had to be found. A simple, practical working language that could be easily assimilated, whilst being effective, was sorely needed.

So, the fundamentals of the 'modern' English were somehow conceived and then spread over the island; and, over the coming centuries, greatly flourished and spread throughout many lands.

So how, then, was this English language invented?

7. Inventing Something Very Simple – English

'English' is a description used quite casually by non-linguistic specialists. In fact, there is considered to be Old English (in reality, Anglo Saxon), Middle English (the newly invented English), and Modern English (which we speak now).

Anglo-Saxon or Saxon is the term given to the various related and similar languages brought to England by the invader-settlers of the Germanic tribes of Angles, Saxons, and Jutes, from about AD 450 onwards (after the Romans had left). The result of this fusion of these north European languages within England is referred to as Anglo-Saxon. It was still a Germanic type language that had very little resemblance to what is English today, and it gradually replaced the language of England's previous indigenous population who spoke Celtic type languages.

This Anglo-Saxon language was also influenced by Old Norse, which was the language brought to England by the invading, and then settling, Vikings; mainly in North England.

Consequently, Anglo-Saxon is the language that was being used in England before the Norman Conquest, and would be quite incomprehensible to the users of modern

English today. It was also incomprehensible to the French speaking Normans when they arrived. Anglo Saxon is described as 'Old English' only because of its location; England. It was, in fact, very much a German language with all the complications of that language.

Just to give a taste of Anglo Saxon and how unlike English it is, see this example of the Lord's Prayer (chosen because the content of the prayer has not changed):

And lead us not into temptation but deliver us from evil = Modern English

And ne gelaed thu us on costnunge ac alys us of yfele sothlice = Anglo Saxon

As you can see, the Anglo Saxon language is very different. We will return to these differences later.

The English language that was created that we begin to recognise as the English we know today, is called Middle English, and manuscripts in this Middle English existed by 1154, which is less than 100 years after the Norman Conquest in 1066. By the 1300s this Middle English had replaced the dominant language of learning, Latin, in most 'schools' and we know that Middle English also replaced French for use of records in the new 'parlements' by 1362. So, within this relatively short time the language we recognise as 'English' had somehow been created and replaced both the old Anglo-Saxon language and Norman-French. Some feat! This creation of a new language was astonishingly fast within the great scheme of human evolution and language evolution. How and why was it created?

The answer is 'necessity'. The French-speaking Normans and the Anglo Saxon speaking Saxons, had to learn to communicate, as much as they disliked each other.

However, we cannot be certain how this creation of modern English happened. Was it an incremental creation, little by little, year on year? Was it in various creative jumps? Was it in one great big creative jump? We don't really know. Except, something happened to create this new and beautifully simple language.

What follows is one possible answer to this language 'creation' mystery. It is imagined, unprovable, and maybe to some readers, an outrageous description of how English was 'invented'. But, the imagined solution does deal with some of the fundamental new creations of English.

Let us start with the question of simplicity. I frequently hear the opinion (always from native English speakers), that English is a difficult language. I don't know where this false belief originated, but it probably arose from wishful thinking as it is comforting to think your own language is 'sophisticated and difficult'. It is completely untrue. In fact, English is an easy and undemanding language in its foundation and essential structures.

You may not be convinced of this, but it is simple, and shortly I will explain how and why it is simple in its structure. The inescapable fact is that it had to be simple to work and be accepted as an effective communication bridge for the two opposed communities of Saxons and Normans. To expect the two communities to bother to learn it, and use it, and spread its use, it had to be simple, there was no choice. It is a compromise between two competing languages: Anglo-Saxon and French; and its grammar is far simpler than either of these two languages.

Now, back to the story of its 'invention'. This is where you have to use your imagination and travel with me, back in time, through the dark, chilly and murky English mists, to an unknown place, somewhere in England in those early medieval times, almost 900 years ago. Probably to a town or village in middle-England? Perhaps somewhere like Warwick, for instance? To a long forgotten monastery, maybe, with high walls and locked gates for security against a difficult and violent world outside. Why a monastery? Well, this might be an acceptably 'neutral' gathering place for Normans and Saxons to meet, and the right place to get the necessary peace and quiet to bring interested parties together and attempt a mammoth task; of devising a new language.

Let us imagine a largish gathering of interested parties in the main building of this shadowy, but secure monastery. Present are probably quite a few learned and hooded clerics of both Saxon and Norman origin, plus some Norman crown 'Officers', like a Sheriff or two, maybe a couple of burly Saxon Earls, a few Saxon merchants, a couple of enlightened Norman aristocrats, and maybe a couple more hardened Norman and Saxon Knights of the realm. The Chairman of this group, who has been personally appointed by the King for this mammoth task, is the monastery's Abbot, possibly someone like the Right Reverend Cedric Pierre La Pointe. He is of high social standing, from an aristocratic Norman father and, very unusually, an aristocratic Saxon mother. Therefore he understands both languages and cultures and, very importantly, knows the importance of building bridges between communities. Needless to say, he has received the very best education available.

These people are assembled with the hugely important and unique task of trying to create a new working language. So, this is going to be a very, very, long meeting (and I mean weeks, even months). The King has ordered it so, and what the King wants, gets done, does it not?

When is this? We don't know precisely, but perhaps it is towards the end of the reign of King Henry 1st, Henry Beauclerc. He is known to have spent most of his early life in England, unlike his war-loving father (William the bastard; sorry, King William), and he may well have been educated by the Anglo Saxon clergy. As King, Henry is less interested in fighting, hunting and being 'bit of a lad' than his father and very obnoxious, but now dead, brother William 'Rufus', and Henry 1st is generally considered to be a harsh but effective administrator, reformer of his realm and skilful politician, even if he does also have some very unpleasant traits in his character. Perhaps he has realised that he must create a more integrated community as an alternative to a nation divided between the sullen Anglo-Saxons and their Norman overlords. The conquest, and all that entailed, is now fading into distant memory (no ever-present media to remind people of past battles, back then) and, with Henry, England has a ruler that is interested in the kingdom, wants it to develop, and he has already adopted much of the existing Anglo-Saxon justice system. Consequently, development and progress requires the ability for his subjects to communicate.

We can only guess when this meeting might have taken place. Around 1130 perhaps? 64 years since the Norman Conquest. Let us listen in on this meeting. Let us be a fly on the wall. Perhaps Latin is used as the language of mediation? Or a mish-mash of Saxon and French? We don't know and can only guess, but to make listening easier, I will translate the meeting's events into modern English so we can all understand ...

The appointed Chairman, Abbot Cedric Pierre, enters the room where the meeting is to be held. He is a large man for his time and has a commanding presence, but he also radiates serenity mixed with determination. He claps his hands to gain attention as he sits at the head of the large, oval oak table prepared for the committee members, who now join the Abbot. The room is well lit with wall torches and candles, and on both sides of the room are large open fires, well fed with large timbers and side-tended by two junior monks (it is late autumn). A couple of very large dogs lay on the scattered rugs in front of one of the fires. There are jugs of water and wine on the table with goblets for the members. In the shadows by the main entrance door to the room, more junior monks standby with large urns of wine and beer to keep the meeting well-oiled for long discussions. In the distance can be heard the melancholy, deep hum of the monastery choir. The atmosphere which is warm and smells of burning apple, feels reassuring. Then the Abbot Chairman starts:

Alright, gentlemen, let us begin, he says in a loud, firm, authoritative voice. We accept and agree that what is needed is a language that is easy enough for your average, not too bright, Saxon peasant or Norman soldier to be able to use. We also know that neither French, nor the existing Saxon language, is acceptable to the separate – ahem – communities. He looks pleased with himself at thinking of the inclusive word, 'communities'. So, he continues. We need some creative thinking, 'outside the moat' you might say, and he looks around smiling expansively, showing his large yellowish teeth. And, gentlemen, this new language needs to be simple. Any ideas, any opinions?

There are mutterings and murmurings around the table. Yes, pipes up someone after a pause of a few seconds, in a voice with what sounds like a mild Welsh accent – if we need such a new language, let's be a bit daring and innovative. Let's take this opportunity to be radical and challenging. Why not? It's not every day you get the chance to invent a new language!

'Ahem', with clearing of the throat – 'Just exactly how should we be innovative?' demands one sceptical voice from across the table.

Well, for instance, why on earth do we have all this male and female stuff for all our things? You know what I mean; our nouns, that all need le or la or les in French, or se, thaet, seo, tha, thone, thaes in Saxon. I have never been able to understand why we need all that complicating noun-gender rubbish. What makes a table or a house 'female', I ask you, and bread and morning 'male', for heaven's sake? It's just ridiculous when you think about it. Why have all this male, female, or even neuter genders for our nouns? For inanimate objects? It just seems ridiculous, unnecessary and makes life terribly complicated.

At first there is a stunned silence from most. Then murmuring and muttering, and some head nodding, and some head shaking. Then more positive nodding and shrugging, and then several voices pipe up with the general message: 'Yes, I suppose he does have a point. It does seem a bit strange when you think about it. Never really thought about it before, but it is a bit odd, all this male and female stuff.'

Alright, says the Chairman, with a look of pleasant surprise in his voice. Now, that is a radical thought, but we are getting somewhere. We are not pulling up the drawbridge on lateral thinking (the Chairman has done some management training recently). I like it. This is a very interesting idea. Although it is a very radical proposal, I do like the idea very much and, therefore, I propose we consider getting rid of gender for nouns and just have 'things' in our new language – things without gender. Nouns with no gender, so everything, all nouns, are just … neutral. No genders, no different word endings. Comment, gentlemen? Any thoughts?

Well, that's all very well, says one sceptical voice (there's always one), but with what do you replace le, la, les, un, une, or thaet, tha, thone, thaes, etc, if we go along with this very radical idea?

Well, says the Chairman, perhaps, we just need one, or maybe two articles to replace them. Perhaps just something like, well, how about 'the' and 'a'? 'the' sounds a bit like 'le' and 'tha', if you shut your eyes and listen, and 'a' sounds a bit like 'un' or 'ein', so we could have: the wall, the woman, the man, the cow, the table, the bread, the morning; or a house, a horse, a walk, a church, a man, a woman. What do you think? Can it work?

Again, there is stunned silence. This suggestion really is very radical. But, it has been proposed! The unthinkable has been suggested. Something so simple. Then people start talking amongst themselves, with animation, with nodding and shaking of heads, and starting to perhaps agree that possibly, just possibly, this can work. This is great progress. After a few minutes, someone shouts "I strongly agree with the learned Abbot's wonderful, ingenious idea." (this, from the Abbot's deputy), and then another agrees, and gradually heads begin to nod, with no apparent disagreement (they are fully aware, of course, the

King is behind this, so have no wish to be seen as obstructive).

Great idea. No gender for things, then. So be it. Beautiful. And simple. I like it.

Like it a lot, blurts out another one of the members (possibly one of the Abbot's many assistants).

Good. Excellent, says the Chairman, feeling mightily pleased with himself and rubbing his hands together in pleasure. We all agree then. And, therefore, that must also mean there is no need for constantly changing adjectives either, does it?

Silence and incomprehension. What do you mean, asks an uncertain voice?

Well, says the Chairman, if we use an example, let's take green, 'vert' in French, we presently use 'vert' for male words, and 'verte' for female words, and verts or vertes for their plurals. In our new system it would be just 'vert' – for everything. No changing adjectives, no changing nouns. Everything stays the same; neutral. No gender. Vert door, vert doors, vert man, vert woman. What do you say? It is the next logical step, and so much easier, is it not?

Another momentary stunned silence, but much shorter than before. Then, "Yes, yes", comes the chorus of approval. Great idea. Love it. Make life simpler. Great idea.

'But I must say, if I may?' up one of the older Saxon monks, in a slightly distressed, plaintive voice, I do prefer the Saxon word 'gron' to the French 'vert'. It's a much nicer word for green.

Yes, yes, yes, says the Chairman (with a note of testy exasperation), alright, alright. It was only an example.

We'll deal with vocabulary later. What about the principle? We get rid of gender for nouns and adjectives? Do we all agree?

Yes, yes. Agreed, agreed, the meeting shout in one voice. Agreed.

So, that was the first great simplification for the new English language. Removing gender from nouns, and all accompanying adjectives and descriptors. One giant step for the new English language, and unique among the wide range of European languages. Simple, but effective.

But – what about verbs, shouts someone? It's those awful verbs I don't like. All those different verb endings. They are such an absolute pain in the … you know what! Which verb endings do we use in this new language, then? The French, or the Saxon verb endings? Always having to decide the right verb ending really does my head in, so it does! It's so complicated. Conjugating they call it. More like conjuring if you ask me.

Silence. Then a large smile spreads across the face of the Chairman. Alright, why not just continue in the direction we have started, he says ('direction' was another management word he had picked up in training and liked). Keep things simple. Why have different endings for the verb forms at all? Instead of different verb endings like: I work, we workons, you workez, they workent – you know what I mean – why not just use 'work' for all the stages of verbs?

There is a feeling of astonishment in the air. You mean, just use I work, you work, he work, we work, they work, asks a disbelieving voice?

Yes, yes, says the Chairman. Exactly. I learn, you learn, he learn, we learn, they learn. Let's keep it simple.

Brilliant, blurts out one of the assembled (probably the Abbot's deputy, again). Why not? It's so easy, so simple, and so logical. Just like getting rid of genders for nouns. Keep it simple. I love it. So clever, Mr Chairman.

Yes, yes; perhaps, says another, with a distinct sceptical tone to his voice. But, before we get too excited and agree, isn't it a bit too simple? Shouldn't there be something to make it a bit more sophisticated, or foreigners might think we are complete morons for using something so absolutely simple? Especially those blasted French know-alls with all their smugness and high and mighty ways (thinking of his own French in-laws).

Yes, blurts another. He has a point. It can't be toooo simple!

Alright, alright, alright, says the Chairman, with some exasperation. Let me think. Let me think. What about, what about, what about if we put 's' on the 'he/she/it' form. So it would be:

I work, you work, we work, they work ... but – wait for it – he, or she, or it ... works!

How about that? Would that satisfy you? We add 's' to the 3rd person, just to prove we are not complete simpletons and make it a bit more sophisticated. However, it's still simple. Do you agree to that?

Another moment of silence, then some muted discussion. Then, a grudging agreement. Alright 's' for the 3rd person. Makes it a little less simple. Don't want people thinking we are complete simpletons. Yes, yes, yes ... We agree. Much nodding around the table.

And, so, it was agreed, the next great simplification. No change of verb endings for all regular verbs (except the dreaded 3rd person 's'). Another great breakthrough was achieved. Verb endings for the new English language would be made simple; at least for the regular verbs.

And what about the past tense then, asks another committee member, with a hint of superiority that slightly irritated the Chairman (who was now really beginning to feel very satisfied about how things were going). How do we put the verbs in the past tense?

After some thought and further debate, it was decided to just use 'ed' (or 't', similar sound) to make regular verbs past tense: I worked, you worked, he worked, we worked, they worked. I learnt, you learnt, we all learnt. Again, simple, simple, simple. The meeting was now definitely on a roll, and the wine and beer was being consumed quite a lot by this stage. It was all very positive, as the Abbot later reported to the King.

And what about the future then? That is a bit more difficult, methinks, said one doubting voice! (They liked words such as 'methinks' back then). The future tense really does have complicated verb endings in our present languages?

Can't see why that should be, shouts out another voice, now slightly slurred by mead. Why not just add something like 'will' before the verb: I will work, you will work, he will work, we will work, they will work. What's wrong with that then? (The meeting had definitely swung in the Chairman's favour, and the wine and mead was going down very well).

Nothing, as far as I can tell, says the Chairman. Sounds fine to me. Though, I must say (he says with some reservation), the future is not always so definite as 'will', in my humble opinion (whether Abbot Cedric Pierre had ever had to be anything remotely resembling 'humble' is highly questionable – but not now).

OK, OK, pipes up another voice, so, how about this. Does this work for you? We give a choice for the future, such as: I will work, I could work, I might work, I should work; or, we should learn, or they might learn, or she ought to learn, and so on. That is less definite about the future, is it not? It gives choice of certainty, but it's still fairly simple.

Well, indeed it is, says the Chairman, a very satisfied Chairman by now. Again, wonderfully simple. I like it. I love it. Simplicity, but with choice. Excellent idea.

After this breakthrough part of the discussion and the simplifying of noun-genders, and verb endings, and tenses, the meeting eventually went on to discuss the much more thorny area of vocabulary; whether to use an existing Saxon word, or an existing Norman word, or a mixture of the two, or something completely different, for each thing. This was a much bigger task, and lasted a lot longer (many weeks, in fact) with some pretty robust discussions, arguments, grudging compromises, fatigue, and some bad hangovers. It was generally (begrudgingly) accepted that, as the Saxons were the majority population, it would be easier, and more easily accepted, if more frequently used words were Saxon in origin; and less used words, but some important words, were French in origin.

It was not an easy negotiation, and often there were compromises. For instance, it was decided that 'haus' would mean ... house; and the French word, 'maison', was rejected. Then it was agreed, after some disagreement, that perhaps some smaller houses could be called 'maisonettes'. A brilliant compromise.

The word green was agreed, very similar to the Saxon gron. But, also accepted that a shade of green could be verdant, similar to the Norman word vert.

In fact, quite often, both the Saxon word and French word were accepted so people could have a choice. For example, the word 'pig' was decided for the farm animal, and it was agreed that cochon was a bit of a mouthful. For some reason, the Saxons hung on grimly to their love of the word 'shwein', and eventually it was agreed that 'swine' could be used as well as pig. This type of compromise seemed to be satisfactory and acceptable to all present. Compromise was the order of the day; most of the time.

But, there were also some odd disagreements. The Normans, for some strange reason, got hung up on the word fourchette, for fork, and would not agree to the Saxon word, until some enterprising Saxon suggested shortening fourchette to 'fork', using the Saxon 'k'. This swung opinion, and it was agreed.

Sometimes French and Anglo Saxon words combined to form a new word, such as the French 'gentil' and the Germanic 'mann' combined to formed gentleman.

Word doublets were also a clever compromise. These were the combination of an Anglo Saxon word, like 'law', and a French word, like 'ordre', to make 'law and order'. The same happened with lord and master, love and cherish, ways and means, for example.

And it went on, hour after hour, day after day, week after week, until a basic working vocabulary was finally thrashed out and agreed.

It was also agreed that some nouns, but only a very few, could be gender-ised, like actor and actress, widow and widower, blond and blonde. This does not seem to have been a problem in being agreed, and it satisfied the desire not to be thought too simple by the contemptuous French.

And, in a nutshell, that was the invention of English, known now as 'Middle English'. Well, probably not in the manner I have described, but somehow it happened, somehow that is what emerged. A greatly simplified compromise language was created, with no gender and different endings for nouns and adjectives; easy regular-verb endings; and a vocabulary that is a mixture of French and Saxon-type words. A brilliantly compromise, or hybrid, that was a melding and simplifying of the two competing languages. Simplicity was the order of the day, and the result was simplicity.

This meeting described obviously did not take place (I don't think). It is clearly a playful invention. However, it is a useful description and summary of the compromise that did somehow emerge, consciously or sub-consciously, to create English. The facts remain the same. English is a simple, practical, working language that can be readily and easily learnt by people in its rudimentary form.

And, though many changes to English have taken place through the centuries, including the so-called Great Vowel Shift between 1400 and 1800 (affecting how vowels are pronounced); and English spelling is, and continues to be, a source of disagreement and irritation within English speaking communities, nevertheless, the basics of the language mean that a new learner of English is not burdened with those tiresome gender differences and complicated verb endings. And that is important when English is competing for dominance and popularity with other languages, because it is simple in its basic structures. People generally like 'easy' to learn, and always will. And, why not?

I'm sure the Saxon peasant and common Norman soldier certainly preferred 'easy'; don't you?

8. English Language Milestones

Putting aside the playful idea of a language-invention committee, what do we know historically and factually about the appearance of the English language as we know it today?

There was no recorder of the progress of English around at the time when it emerged, unfortunately. Probably because, like now, language was just happening, all around. It was not a big news event. There were no such people as linguistic specialists; in fact there weren't even 'academics' as we know them today. There weren't universities observing the world and doing doctoral theses on subjects like linguistics. The English language was simply evolving and developing, rapidly in comparison with past languages, but it wasn't exactly front page news back then.

However, we do have some very useful pieces of evidence about the emergence of English. The Anglo-Saxon Chronicles are an invaluable source of very helpful evidence. Despite all that very unpleasant business with William the Conqueror and his nasty Norman cronies and eldest son William Rufus, of conquering, pillaging and ravaging; life did go on as normal in many places and in many ways. And, to our great advantage, in some places, such as monasteries, so did the production of the Anglo Saxon Chronicles carry on for some considerable time after the conquest of 1066.

The chronicles had always been written in Anglo Saxon by order of King Alfred when they began in about 890 AD. Then, in 1154, which is 88 years after the Normans arrived, the Peterborough Chronicle, produced in Peterborough Abbey, suddenly switched to using English as we call it today. Suddenly, a recognisable form of our modern English appears.

What is very interesting is that the first parts of this Peterborough Chronicle were written in Anglo Saxon, as expected, and then in 1154 its writing abruptly changed to English (the Peterborough Chronicle was written between 1070 and 1154). It was a clearly identifiable change in the language used.

Now, that sudden switch in use of language is very interesting, is it not? What caused this sudden switch in language? Obviously the new 'writer' would have been some hard working monk used as a scribe, but his predecessors had always written in Anglo-Saxon, and this new scribe is now writing in English, seated on his high stool with only a candle to work by. We can only speculate why this sudden change happened, but it does tell us two things.

The first is that the new writer can obviously speak this new English language to be able to write it. Secondly, he must have been given permission to use this new English language by the Abbot of Peterborough. So, it means that the new monk-scribe had had time to learn, or be taught, the new language. And, it also suggests that English was now so widely used that the Abbot felt fit to give permission to use it. Let's face it, Abbots were not known for their trendy, radical liberal ways, so English must have become acceptable by 1154.

Going back to the new scribe-monk, let's assume he has learnt English as a young person, let's guess 15 years prior to his writings in 1154, in about 1139. 1139 is 73 years after the Norman conquest of 1066. This Peterborough Chronicle is written proof that English, as we recognise it, has well and truly appeared on the scene since 1066, and in less than three generations. That is fast. That is very fast, for a new language to appear.

Was that meeting back in that middle England Abbey, chaired by Abbot Cedric Pierre to create a new language, such a bizarre idea after all? Is it completely fanciful to think that the new language committee may have had the King's permission, or even urging, and that Cedric Pierre – who would have been quite a big cheese in the Abbot world to have the King's ear – could have then gone on to convince his brother Abbots, including the Abbot of Peterborough, of the practical usefulness of this new creation? Hmmm. Makes you think.

Now, what you also need to realise – which is difficult to imagine in these egalitarian and democratic days of the 21st century – is that the aristocracy and nobles back then really did not mix at all with the common proles; the likes of you and me. And, the proles did not write, or have much say in anything important. None of this modern democratic voting back then. Those Norman nobles really did do their own thing. They were very, very powerful and important, and everything that they did was watched very carefully and emulated by their lower nobles.

These aristocratic types were definitely not doing what the commoner did, back then in the 1100s. They were still speaking French and being very clever and sophisticated, and reading in Latin if they had a bit of education (though not many did, as they much preferred pillaging, hunting, drinking and rousting – the normal boy's stuff – to bother with education). So their 'courts', their close followers and attendants, copied them and also spoke French. And, so, two parallel language worlds existed. The common majority were switching to English, fast, from what we now know; whereas their masters carried on regardless in their elitist way, with their French language.

But, 'leakage' was beginning to occur between the classes. From the early 1100s, and for the next 200 years in the Royal Courts of Justice, for example, the language used for business was tri-lingual. French was used for formal proceedings, Latin was used for written records, and informal verbal exchanges with witnesses were occurring more and more in English. Meanwhile, in the manorial courts (like the magistrate's courts of today), English was becoming the normal language of use. So you had these two parallel languages in use – English by the bulk of the population, and Norman French by the ruling classes. Nonetheless, leakage of English into the language of the ruling classes was happening.

Then, in 1204, the unfortunate and inept King John managed to lose Normandy to the French. Normandy was special, as it was Norman, the old country to the Normans and had been part of the family, so to speak, for the past 140 years, ever since King John's ancestor, William of Normandy, had conquered the Anglo Saxons in 1066. This loss of Normandy in France represented the final split for the Anglo-Normans from their French old country heritage, and was another nail in the coffin for the use of the French language in England. In the lower-higher social orders (the upper middle classes), it was becoming less common to tempt a French lady over from France to marry, so inter-marriage was occurring more frequently between Normans and Anglo-Saxons.

All this meant that whilst the Saxon general public were merrily switching languages, or had already switched to this rather practical and easy-to-use English, the upper orders in their castles and keeps, were changing very much more slowly. In fact, at a snail's pace. However, the snail was accelerating a bit.

Then a really big event changed matters completely. The big event was the 100 year war with the French that kicked off in 1337, and actually lasted for 116 years. This began to have an increasing effect on the upper social orders, and the French were no longer 'Top of the Pops' but really quite disliked, and their 'foreign' language, French ... well, its use started to become a little bit suspect and definitely 'infra dig'. More and more of the lower nobility and gentry started to favour English to avoid any hint of being pro French. By 1362, we know that parlements (forerunner of parliament), were beginning to keep records in English.

Then came along Chaucer and Wycliffe. Chaucer was the big beast of literature in his day and something of a celebrity when, with the help of the newly invented printing press, he wrote his classic book 'Canterbury Tales', in English, in 1386. That was a big event. We now have the first printed popular book circulating in England, and its language is English.

Almost at the same time, in fact two years earlier in 1384, John Wycliffe produced his version of the bible in vernacular English (English as spoken by the common man). Wycliffe was a very learned, religious rebel, who was doing and saying all sorts of things that the established church (Roman Catholic) didn't like, and he was increasingly irritating them quite considerably. The church was seen as more and more out of touch, and the traditional services and the bible were, still, all in Latin. Wycliffe's English bible was banned from churches, but it was known to continue to circulate unofficially. So, with Chaucer's 'Tales' and Wycliffe's Bible, both in English, this underpinned the fact that English was well and truly becoming established, and replacing French and Latin.

In 1399 England got a new King, Henry IV, and he was the first king to make his Sovereign Oath in English. And that was it. English was here to stay and the new language was well and truly established throughout all social classes of England. In fact, his son Henry V both spoke and wrote in English.

In the upper echelons, they did cling on to some remnants of the old language. Norman-French used nouns followed by adjectives ('look at that door green'), but English is reversed and uses adjectives followed by nouns ('look at that green door'). The Anglo-Norman aristocracy were still very snooty about certain legal terms and insisted in keeping their reverse order in some legal terms, such as in attorney general, heir apparent, court martial; just to make a point to the vulgar Saxon peasants, perhaps?

Having described the events of the English language gaining ground and becoming established in England, here are the main historical events, listed chronologically:

1066 - Conquest of England by French speaking Normans

1154 - Peterborough Chronicle changes from using Anglo-Saxon to Middle English

1100s–1400s - Royal Law Courts use Latin for writing, French formally, but English informally between lawyers and witnesses. All lower courts (manorial courts) use English

1204 - King John loses Normandy to French

1200s onwards - Intermarriages with 'Saxons' more frequent for Norman nobility. French now more widely used in upper echelons as a 2nd language

1337 - 100 year war with France makes French unpopular. English now used in Public Schools

1362 - Parlements sometimes use English for records

1384 - Wycliffe's bible in vernacular English

1386 - Chaucer uses English for Canterbury Tales

1399 - Henry IV, 1st king to use English as mother tongue, takes Royal Oath in English

1413 - Henry V (Agincourt and all that) also uses English for writing

1400s - Parliament using English for legislation

End of 1400s - French only used by some elite. Most people using English. Modern English now 'in'

1500 onwards - Today's modern English now readily recognisable

Where does this information about its progress leave the question 'when was English created?' Well, if you take the Peterborough Chronicle, it would be entirely reasonable to suggest that English (Middle English), with its new simplicity, had been invented within 75 years following the Norman invasion. That is extremely fast.

However, it is one thing to create a new language, but another thing to have it widely accepted.

It might be useful to readers at this point to give actual examples of Anglo Saxon, Middle English, and Modern English, so a comparison can be made. Look again at this line below taken from the Lord's Prayer. The first line is Modern English and will be easily recognised. Under it is written the same line in Middle English:

And lead us not into temptation but deliver us from evil = Modern English

And lede us not into temptacion but delyuere us from euyl = Middle English

There are spelling differences between Middle English and Modern English. 'U' was used for v (still is in some languages), y was used as 'i/I' sound (still is in filly, dirty, etc), but this Middle English is readily recognisable as 'English', I think you will agree?

Now look again at this same line in Anglo Saxon:

And ne gelaed thu us on costnunge ac alys us of yfele sothlice

We can recognise 'and', 'us', 'of', but I think you will agree it is pretty incomprehensible, and a long way from the Middle English shown above.

The vast difference between Anglo Saxon and Middle/Modern English is again illustrated in this line from a poem which is about the 'Battle of Maldon' 991 (Saxons versus Vikings)

But I by the side of my lord, be he so dear a man, intend to lie = English translation

Ac ic me be healfe minum hlaforde, be swa leofum menn, licgan þence. = Anglo Saxon

The Anglo Saxon language is pretty incomprehensible, is it not? You can work out that 'ac' means 'but', 'ic' is I, 'be' is by, and 'menn' is man, but otherwise, incomprehensible. (In case you are interested, the battle was in coastal Essex and a victory to the Vikings, the Saxons losing comprehensibly. Aethelred, The Unready, was the Saxon King of England at the time; oh dear, perhaps the clue to his lack of success is in the name!).

So, back to the question of when was English created. The answer is probably between 1066 and 1154. Rather than ask when it was invented, if you would rather ask the question 'when was English firmly established in England?', I would say by the mid-1200s, which is still only about 175 years after 1066. That, in terms of language creation, is still pretty fast.

Whether you choose the Peterborough Chronicle as your marker, 88 years after 1066; or Chaucer using English later as a popular text, there is no denying that a new, practical, simple language had been created really quite quickly in terms of normal language evolution. And that was no mean accomplishment, wouldn't you agree?

9. English Regulation. Not on Your Life!

Having been invented, how was the English language regulated?

The answer is: it is most definitely not regulated and never has been. There is no institution that tries to regulate the English language, and this is one of the secret strengths of English. It is a free-market language.

This lack of regulation is very different to other main languages. The French have their *Academie francaise* to regulate the French language, which they take very seriously. The Spanish have their *Asociacion de Acadamias de la lengua Espanola*. The Germans have their *Council for Orthography* (orthography is the study of spelling). The Italians have their *Accademia della Crusca*. The Chinese have their *National Commission on Language and Script*. Even small countries like Serbia have a *Board for Standardisation of the Serbian language*!

If you internet search to see the list of 'Language Regulators', you will find 108 languages listed, with regulatory bodies responsible for languages ranging from Afrikaans to Yiddish, with most main languages listed. But not English.

This lack of regulation is very typically English. The English instinctively dislike regulation, whether it be in business, in personal life (such as refusing to have identity cards), policing, and government. The Anglo-Saxon, English person, British person, Australian, Canadian, New Zealand and American person, all have an instinctive disdain and dislike of regulation. In short, we English speakers are an awkward lot who don't like being told what to do. This lack of 'respect' for regulation and bureaucracy is still very prevalent today and scorned by many continental countries, especially France, as the 'Anglo Saxon' way.

But, hereby lies one of the many strengths of English. We don't want English regulated, so nobody tries (well, maybe a few frustrated grammarians). It is owned by the world, the free market, and the world can take what it wants, and give what it wants, to the English language. We, the English speaking population, will decide if we want to use new words and new formations, not some central, interfering, governmental regulatory body. It is this lack of regulation that has helped the English language flourish, and have freedom from interference and regulation. We readily change our language and rapidly adapt foreign words if they fill a gap in our vocabulary arsenal. We don't want regulation. We do accept precedence (for grammar), but are ready to change the precedence if necessary, as we do our laws and constitution. If it works, it is practical and it is acceptable, why not?

The nearest thing approaching any form of English language guidance is the Oxford English Dictionary (usually referred to as the OED). The OED has staff that, each year, examine their famous dictionary and decide if new words merit a place in their book because they are being widely used and understood, or decide if other words have lapsed into non-use and should be removed, though they have no power outside the reference of the dictionary. One can choose, or not choose, to refer to the OED. It is a matter of personal choice. In the USA, Webster's dictionary serves a similar purpose. In Britain, the BBC is often considered as being a pseudo authority on pronunciation, though it has no official status for this role. This complete lack of official, central regulation is, paradoxically, one of the English language's greatest strengths.

Those vocal antagonists to the English language, the French, have never realised this freedom from regulation is one of the secrets of success for English. The French love their own language, understandably, but they also love regulations and the Napoleonic Code approach to many matters. Their *Academie francaise* was established almost four centuries ago in 1635, long before the English even tried to write an English Dictionary (Dr Johnson published his English dictionary in 1755, wonderfully portrayed in the Blackadder 3rd series; a 'must watch' episode if you have not done so). So, the French have been regulating their language, in their inimitable way, for a long time. And, with regulation and control invariably comes inflexibility.

The French authorities openly dislike and resist the invasion of foreign words, especially English words, into their protected language (such as 'le weekend', 'le squash'), and want to regulate and restrict, and to prevent pollution of their language which they jealously guard.

And they wonder why they are left on the side-lines of language globalisation and bewail the relentless progress of the barbaric 'Anglais' language. They cannot comprehend why their lovely French language is not the first global language of choice as they feel it should be. This is not sarcasm, as French is a lovely language and, of course, an important contributor to the English language, though in a very much simplified form. However, it is not as simple as English and it is not as free spirited as English.

Meanwhile, our English language has no masters, no authority to rein in its additions, its expansion, its development, its restlessness, and some might say, distortion. It is one of the English language's best kept little secrets. English operates and develops with freedom.

English roams around the world, absorbing new vocabulary from different regions of the globe. From China, it absorbed the word ketchup. From Malaysia, sago and gong. From India and South Asia, the lexical delights of curry, shawl, bungalow, dungarees, shampoo, pyjamas, and chutney. From the Americas we adopted potato, chocolate, tomato, and puma. And from the Arabian countries we used coffee, alcoves, sequins, and giraffes. These are just a very few examples of vocabulary absorption at which English excels.

This freedom means English can readily adapt its form to whoever wants to use it, wherever and whenever. It is the chameleon of languages, and such flexibility chimes extremely well in these changing times of the 21st century. It has many forms and some strange forms, such as Pidgin English, and some difficult-to-understand dialects. In its original home, England, there are still many dialects and vernacular forms to be heard. Some would say, sadly, these dialects seem to be reducing in their differentiation, probably because of the influence of television, radio, and population mobility.

There is no shortage of self-appointed guardians of the English language. Letters to newspapers, battling over a wide range of perceived linguistic 'crimes', can be fierce and unforgiving over the most obscure grammar or vocabulary aberrations in the use of English. Such battles are usually a bit silly, but do prompt many opinions. If a range of English literature is examined over the centuries since Shakespeare and Donne, it soon becomes obvious that spelling, vocabulary, punctuation, and grammar itself, is forever changing, and has varied significantly over time and between authors. This is how it should be; a language constantly developing, improving, changing and adapting to the times and places in which it finds itself. We cannot, and should not, try to 'freeze' English now and state this is how it should be used. English is dynamic, and not written in stone.

A completely free market for English existed in its entirety until Dr Johnson came along with his dictionary in 1755, and this seemed to be the spark that started grammarian passions. Since that time certain 'rules' have been invented, challenged, and often de-invented. One notable example is the perceived grammar 'rule' that a verb's infinitive form should not be split. The infinitive is the root form of a verb; for instance: to work, to go, to say, to learn. The rule that someone, somewhere, dreamt up is that no word should intervene between 'to' and the verb, in other words not to split to + verb. This apparent rule of not splitting the infinitive seems to have been generally and passively accepted by those that care for such things, like grammarians and old-style English teachers. That is until the hugely popular 'Star Trek' series came to television screens some decades ago. The introduction to each programme was a dramatic American voice stating that: *"These are the voyages of the Star-ship Enterprise. Its 5-year mission: to explore strange new worlds, to seek out new life and new civilizations, **to boldly go** where no man has gone before."*

The provocative words that caused all the linguistic anguish and gnashing of teeth, making grammarians go hot under the collar, are written in bold above. It is "To boldly go" that caused all the fuss and grammarians sleepless nights. It should say, the grammar police insisted, "To go boldly ..." The infinitive should not be split under any circumstances, in this case 'boldly' intruding between 'to and go'. This was a heinous grammar crime that would pollute a generation of impressionable Star Trek enthusiasts, and possibly bring the English language to its very knees.

I suspect that, as well as infuriating the ever vigilant English grammar police, such a great fuss was also motivated by a tad of anti-Americanism that is just below the surface for some English language academics. This was all much ado about nothing and the accusation that this grammar crime was a symptom of a lazy, poorly educated, new generation really did not hold water. The words of one of our greatest authors, George Bernard Shaw (again), had obviously been forgotten. He had written to The Times newspaper early in the 20th century, before World War 1, and many decades prior to Star Trek, saying:

"There is a busybody on your staff who devotes a lot of time to chasing split infinitives: I call for the immediate dismissal of this pedant. It is of no consequence whether he decides to go quickly or to quickly go, or quickly to go. The important thing is that he should go at once."

The fact is, that whilst English grammar books do exist, and can be useful for learning and teaching English, and also provide useful and helpful advice for language guidance, there is no authority in existence to either decide upon, monitor, or enforce any grammar rules for English. What a grammarian thinks about splitting the infinitive, or any other grammar aberration, is simply their opinion, with no body of enforcement or even arbitration available. Grammar 'rules' are there to be broken, changed, challenged and distorted, at will. Regulation of the English language does not exist outside the English classroom, or a newspaper editor's office. And long may it remain so.

There is a difference, though, between pedantic grammar rules with no real substance and no useful contribution; and useful grammar guidance and precedence to help us use clear, unambiguous English. We will return to some grammar later in this book (not too much, I hasten to assure you). It is worth remembering that grammar 'rules' should only be obeyed if it helps make English easier to understand, and helps avoid confusion for the reader (or listener).

10. How Many People in the World Use English?

Skip this chapter if you are not interested in numbers and statistics. Numbers are not everybody's cup of tea and, if you are one of those people, it is understandable if you don't want to wrestle with these numbers and explanations. That said, there is more to this chapter than just numbers. This chapter explains the different categories of people that speak English, which is interesting in itself and explains how some of these categories are very difficult to quantify. The chapter concludes that probably about 15–25% of the world's population now speak English to some degree of reasonable competence, but it is impossible to verify these numbers with any accuracy. In addition, it explains that English is the most widely spoken language in the world. However, if you are interested in knowing more about how many people use English, I have tried to make the explanation not too dry …

How many people in the world today presently speak or use English? It may seem on the surface an easy question, but it's certainly not easy to answer. In fact, it is a very difficult question to answer. There are no central authorities keeping a record of how many people can speak

English, so we have to dig and research and guesstimate where necessary, using whatever evidence is available.

Firstly, it depends what is meant by 'speak' or 'use' English. Speaking or using any language, including English, can have a very wide spread of competence, and varies from being used constantly and fluently, such as by a native-English-speaker; to being used only occasionally in a very basic manner. Where possible to judge competence by accepted standards, I would turn to the definition use by the Cambridge University First Certificate examination in English which uses the criteria of '*understandable use of English in familiar situations*'. However, there are many users of English, probably many who can use English but have not done an international exam in English. So, judging competence becomes something of a subjective judgement, or even a guessing game!

There are countries, like the USA, UK, Australia, Canada, New Zealand in which English is the natural and principal language of the population. Then there are those countries in which English is not the natural 1st language, but English is still the 'official language' for use within government and education. India is such an example. This 'official' category makes a huge difference when trying to count how many people use English.

In addition, there are those countries in which English is not used either naturally or officially, but is learned by a substantial proportion of the population to a credible, or even good level of competence. Sweden is a good example. It is more possible to get a reasonable number for these people, but it is still not that accurate.

And, because central records and surveys in some countries are very poor, if available at all, or the country is very closed to outside scrutiny, there can never be an accurate answer for the total of all these categories. I will try to give a sensible, practical and realistic answer to the question: How many English speakers are there in the world today? – based on whatever evidence does exist, reports from some credible sources, and my own experience.

So, bear with my explanations for a short while and I will try my best to come up with some realistic numbers. You may be interested in discovering that there are these different categories of English speakers.

English as 1ˢᵗ natural language, or mother tongue

The categorisation of people that speak English as their 1st and natural language, or mother tongue, is the easiest category to recognise and quantify, because most of these countries are highly developed countries with good records of their population.

The total native-English-speaking population in this category is said by Ethnologue to be 372 million, and this makes English the 3rd most-spoken 'native' language (**Ethnologue**: Languages of the World, is a web-based publication that contains information about the world's living languages). Chinese is by far the most-spoken native language, followed by Spanish, followed by English. The table from *Ethnologue*, 2017, gives this information:

Language	speakers
1. Chinese	1,284,000,000

2. Spanish	437,000,000
3. English	**372,000,000**
4. Arabic	295,000,000
5. Hindi	260,000,000
6. Bengali	242,000,000
7. Portuguese	219,000,000

Source Ethnologue 2017.
https://www.ethnologue.com/statistics/size

The 372 million native-English-speakers includes those countries where English is the natural 1st language and includes all the obvious candidates: USA, UK, Canada, Australia, Ireland, New Zealand …

But does this total mean anything in terms of our question, how many people in the world use English competently? I'm afraid not, really, because English is much more widely used than this category of native speakers, so this number is only the part of the iceberg that readily shows itself. There are many more 'hidden' English speakers which are much more difficult to count.

English as the official language (de jure) but not native language

There are countries that count English as their 'official' language for government, education, and the law, even though English is not the 'native' spoken language. The numbers in this group are difficult to estimate.

This use of English as the official language is known as '*de jure* official', *de jure* simply means 'by law', and some countries that have this official use of English include many that you can probably readily name such as India, Pakistan, South Africa, Nigeria, Uganda, Malta, Trinidad, Ghana, Zimbabwe. Then there are some mild surprises such as Singapore, Cameroon, and St Lucia. And, then there are considerable surprises, such as the Philippines, for example.

There are as many as 56 countries listed as having English as their official 'de jure' language, with populations together totalling approximately 2.1 billion people (2,100 million), which is a huge number, and about 28% of the world's population. Unfortunately, there are some difficulties here. In this 'de jure' group are very large countries, and the largest, by far, is India. English is their official language of government and education, but it is not their primary language. There are numerous local languages in India, including Hindi (shown in the table above), and we know that by no means can all the people in India speak English. So that begs the question, how many of the 1250m population of India actually participate in education, or deal with the government, and can speak competent English? It is impossible to know as there are simply no records. The same can be said of Pakistan, also on the 'de Jure' list, with a further 165 million people.

Another very large country where English is 'de jure official' is Nigeria. The population is listed as 218 million, and the primary language is listed as English. Nigeria is a country that I have visited and travelled more than once in recent years. Firstly, it is widely believed that their population count is significantly suspect (that is, low) for a variety of reasons. Secondly, when visiting Nigeria one can hear many local languages being spoken. Certainly in the cities, English is widely spoken; but with a twist. As a visitor I have been spoken to by local Nigerians in perfectly understandable English, but the two Nigerians that speak this understandable English will then switch to speaking to each other in a rapid pidgin English that is difficult to understand for most native-English-speakers.

Pidgin is a grammatically simplified form of a language, often combined with local language words. Pidgin language eventually becomes 'creole'. Creole originates from pidgin, and then is further developed in its vocabulary, and there are significant pronunciation and grammar differences from the original language. Today there are over 60 English creole languages, used by up to 200 million people, and they can be almost impenetrable to native-English-speakers. It is difficult to know if these creole versions should be included as English, and how many of these speakers can switch to 'normal' English as needed.

A big surprise on this list of official English speaking countries is The Philippines, an ex-Spanish colony. I imagine most people would think that a Spanish type language dominates in the Philippines (in addition to local dialects) but, in fact, their official languages are Filipino and English. Spanish, which is not an official language there, has almost disappeared over the past century. Of this large population of 100 million, how many Filipinos actually speak English competently, I wonder? Again, there are no records kept.

It is obvious that some proportion of this cohort of 'de jure official' English speaking populations must be included as competent English language users, but the actual number is very difficult to estimate with any accuracy or confidence, and I can find no research or comment to give a reassuring estimate.

If we take the total 'official de jure' population of 2100 million and assume or guess that 15% of this total has competent English (I believe it might be more but I apply the rule of prudence) this gives us a total of 315 million. So, we now can increase the Ethnologue total of 372 million English speakers to 687 million.

English as the official language in practice (de facto), though not the native language

In addition to the official '*de jure*' list of 56 countries discussed above, there are five countries where English is not the primary language but is official '*de facto*' (means 'in practice'). These countries are:

Israel, Malaysia, Brunei, Sri Lanka, and the very large Bangladesh.

The combined total populations of these countries is 209 million. Once again, though, knowing how many of their population can actually use English competently is impossible to know. My instinctive guess would be about 50% (100 million), but there is no way of estimating accurately.

Assuming this figure of 100 million, and adding it to the previous calculated total of 687 million, we now have 787 million competent English speakers.

Total of 'official' English language users in the world

You can see the problem we have when counting official English-speaking populations. Taking the numbers described so far and leaving 'competence' aside, and taking these numbers at face value, means totalling:

The native speaking countries with 372m, +

The *de jure* list of 2100m, +

The *de facto* list of 209m

Which gives a total of about 2,681 million people (2.6 billion).

Assuming a present world total population of approximately 7.3 billion people, this means if we accepted this total of 2.6 billion, 35% of the world are classed as officially speaking English.

This is clearly not the case, and I do not claim that 35% of the world's population actually speak or use English competently. You can see the problem of trying to calculate a realistic figure with any degree of accuracy, though. If I now use my own estimate for a 15% proportion of official 'de jure' speakers, plus a 50% proportion of 'de facto' speakers, plus the Ethnologue number of natural English speakers, the total becomes 315m+100m+372m = 787 million. I believe this figure to be conservative.

In 2006, a widely recognised academic specialist in linguistics estimated that there were 400 million native-English-speakers and another 400 million that use English as an official second language. So, that is a total of 800 million. Is this figure credible in the light of change since 2006? I have no idea. This figure is already 11 years out of date at the time of writing. However, at least this 2006 estimate of 800 million comes close to my own present guesstimate of 787 million.

Total figures are often estimated by taking samples of populations, finding percentages (that speak English, for example), and then extrapolating the sample numbers to the whole population. With such large populations, in chaotic and diverse countries like India, Pakistan, Nigeria, and Bangladesh, where even total population counts are dubious, can such extrapolation really work? How credible are these calculations?

English learners in countries not using English as an official language

So far, we have dealt with English users in native-English-speaking countries (USA, UK, etc.), or listed as 'officially' speaking English (India, Zimbabwe, Israel, etc.). So, we now have a guesstimated total of about 800 million, speaking competent English.

But what about those English users that are not native-English-speakers nor live in countries that speak English 'officially'? There are many countries where English is studied very seriously, often compulsorily, in schools. Here I will rely on my own observations and anecdotal evidence gained from involvement in the teaching and examining of English as a foreign language, as I have not been able to find any estimates of their totals, and I am sure it would be an almost impossible task.

Within Europe, many of the 'east European' countries when totalled together have very significant populations, and many have English as a compulsory language from the start to finish of school. Many readers will have heard the competence in English of many east Europeans that travel outside their own countries. They often speak good English, sometimes to quite a high standard. In addition to the East Europeans in the EU, the Russian Federation also has a good level of English, as it is also taught in their schools.

In addition, many of the north European countries have an excellent English language learning regime, such as in Norway, Sweden, Denmark, Netherlands, and Germany, for instance. A high proportion of their population speak English to a good or high standard.

Then there are surprises to be found in countries where you don't expect a good knowledge of English. Italy and Spain are good examples of such surprises. These two countries were, in the past, well-known for not taking much interest in the English language. This was totally understandable. Spanish is a world language in its own right, for example, so why should the Spanish bother learning English, except to cope with tourists.

Italy has no colonial history, and what would be their motivation for learning English when they are geographically surrounded by French speaking, German speaking, and Slavic speaking neighbours? But, much to everyone's surprise, the Italians changed their education policy quite a few years ago and now their school-children are taught English in most schools from a young age.

More surprisingly, in more recent times, Spain has undergone a 'mini revolution' in their attitude to teaching English, and not only is it now a compulsory subject in their schools, but some other subjects in Spanish schools are to be actually taught in English! In recent times, UK has experienced a flood of Spanish teachers wanting and needing to improve their English to comply with the new rules.

You can see the numbers of competent English speakers are beginning to add up. Now I turn to my experience as an English language examiner for a world-wide examination organisation. In recent years, the Chinese, South Koreans, and many South American countries, including Mexico, have been the nationalities dominating these English exams numerically. They are taking internationally recognised English exams each year in their many thousands.

Fifteen to twenty years ago, not many Chinese (of mainland China) did these English exams. In fact, examinees from there were quite unusual. Well, this has now changed in recent decades. They now are the main single-country source of examinees. And, the Chinese and Koreans are travelling to the UK (and America) in their thousands to learn English, in addition to the many thousands learning back in their own country.

These are big countries (such as China and Mexico). And their standard of English, as judged by the exams they are successfully sitting, is steadily improving year on year. Japan is another large country (127 million) in which learning English is taken seriously, though they tend to use their own national exams, or sometimes US exams. I don't know their total numbers of English speakers, but a lot of Japanese can speak competent English.

In China, schoolchildren, at least in the main urban areas, are taught English from their 3rd year in primary school. There are over 50,000 English language schools in China and the Chinese collectively spend huge sums learning English. It is estimated that about one third of China's population are English learners, which is about 400 million people. This is an impressive number, though the critically important key is in the word 'learner'. Learner does not mean competent (able to communicate effectively in familiar situations). I would ask you, for instance, how many English schoolchildren and adults that have learnt French, as one example, over quite a long period of time, class themselves as competent users?

As there is no central registry of the numbers of English students in non-English speaking countries, and there probably never will be, it is quite impossible to estimate an accurate, or even near accurate total of this English speaking cohort, but it is very safe to say quite a few, and ever increasing numbers, have some degree of competence in English.

Taking the countries or regions of: China, the EU countries, Mexico, Indonesia, Brazil, Turkey, Russia, Japan, Egypt, which totals about 2800 million, my own conservative guess for the total number of people that have the ability to use English to a reasonable level of competence would be about 400 million people, but I cannot prove it. I can only use my experience of being in the business and taking an interest in the subject, being an English language examiner, and talking to other people in the business about the growth in language schools and general interest in learning English.

The total number of competent English speakers in the World

I hope the above explanations and definitions of English users have shown how difficult this question of 'what is the number of people in the world that use English competently' is to answer. But, I need to try, to satisfy you, the reader, as wishy-washy excuses are not acceptable. I understand, and will try to answer.

Before we return to the numbers, we have to accept that qualitatively defining English users as 'competent users', or 'useful level' users (British Council description) is difficult and a very subjective guess. That is why I quote my experience as an examiner to try to estimate growth in demand, rather than absolute numbers, because at least there is an element of objectivity to observing growth. It is easier to see that a car is accelerating rather than to guess its speed.

Coming to the numbers, the categories of English users are like the zones of an archery target in that, at the centre, are hard, or more reliable numbers, but the numbers become increasingly soft, or more unreliable, as we move away from the centre.

At the centre, equivalent to the bulls-eye, are the native English speakers otherwise known as 1st language speakers, or mother tongue English speakers. This total is relatively straightforward and is in the range of 372–400 million.

Next we have the 'official' de jure and de facto speakers, sometimes referred to as the 2nd language users. We are now into the guesstimate business and the estimated range here is 400–415 million, though I do think this is conservative, or prudent.

Finally, we have the category of English learners in non-native or non-official English speaking countries, and I readily admit these totals are guesses. What is particularly difficult about this category is that we have highly organised and open societies like the Swedish, Dutch, Spanish countries with their experiences of learning English, alongside much larger and less organised countries such as Philippines and Mexico, or quite close societies like China. Of this category, my guess is about 400 million use English to a competent level.

If my estimates described above are anywhere near accurate, it means that about 1200 million of the world's population now have competent use of English either as a 1st language, or 2nd, or learnt language. This estimate of 1200 million of the world's population makes English the second most popular language used in the world, just below Chinese (1284 million), and translates as 15% of the world's population.

The British Council use a different figure. The British Council is a partly government-funded organisation, loosely associated with the Foreign Office, with offices all around the world, and often has its own language schools in those countries. It printed a booklet on-line in 2013, called 'The English Effect', which seems to have as its main objective the promotion of English language teaching and learning. In this booklet it quite startlingly makes the assertion that some 1.75 billion people speak English at a 'useful level', which is one in four of the world's population, or 25%. There is no explanation of the definition of 'useful level', nor of the figures it proclaims. However, this is a prestigious organisation, with its own language schools, that also examine English learners world-wide as the contractors for an equally prestigious examining organisation, so it is difficult to ignore such an assertion of 25%.

'Ethnologue' is a linguistic service based in Texas, USA that studies languages of the world to determine how many bibles are needed in different languages. So, it is a non-university type institution, and therefore its findings are not tested with the same rigour as university research. Nonetheless, it is one of the few sources of information available concerned with how many people speak English.

According to the Ethnologue, there are almost one billion speakers of English as a 1st or 2nd language. They do not make any visible attempt to estimate the English users in non-1st or 2nd language English speaking countries, but their figure of one billion is not far from my own estimate of 800 million, and if added to the guessed number of competent speakers in non-official English speaking countries, the total is 1.4 billion, or 19% of the world's population.

So now we have three numbers for estimates of the world speaking (competent) English, which is 15% (me), 19% (Ethnologue + me), and 25% (British Council). That is an interesting spread of percentages which translates into a difference of about 730 million people between the top and bottom of the range. A lot of people. So what figure do you, the reader, accept? The British Council certainly have a lot of prestige, but do not give any explanation of their estimate (I have asked them, unsuccessfully). Perhaps it is time to think about the use of English around the world differently. Ethnologue states that English "*…is used for more purposes than any other language.*" Which brings us onto the concept of language spread.

Leaving aside the total population numbers we have been playing with, let us look at the 'spread' of English in terms of the range of countries around the world where it is used. Ethnologue states that out of the total 195 countries in the world, 67 nations have English as the language of 'official status', plus there are also 27 countries where English is spoken as a secondary 'official' language. That is 94 countries of the 195 countries which equals 48% of the world's countries. North Carolina

University, a public research university, counts 54 countries that have English as a second language, as do Wikipedia, plus the 27 countries where English is a secondary official language. That means 41% of the world's countries. So, once again, some difference between the figures, but even so, both 48% and 41% are impressive spreads.

In estimating the extent to which English is spoken in the world, whether you want to look to the population numbers, (my guesstimate of 15% or the British Council's 25%) or the number of countries where English has some official status (41–48%), the use of English throughout the world is pretty impressive when you consider the number of languages that are thought to exist.

For English to be the principal world language, is quite an achievement and a long way from the very small numbers using English 850 years ago, back in the small island of England, with its puny population numbers, on the fringes of north Europe. I'm sure that Abbot Cedric Pierre would have felt particularly pleased with himself if he could have known where his language committee's efforts would lead one day. Wouldn't most people?

11. Why Is English Spreading around the World?

I have explained that a lot of the world's population is now speaking English to some level of competency, and whilst the native-English-speaking population does not have the huge population of the Chinese, English is now the most widely spread language in the world. Its expansion seems to continue, remorselessly, year on year, and from my own experience its use seems to be accelerating. Why is this expansion happening? What is powering this growth?

I think there are many reasons. Despite the assertion of some that it is all due to the Americans, or all due to the Internet, or all due to globalisation, I don't believe that any single reason has caused this incredible growth. Rather, it is a magical combination of factors, such as: English language attributes (simplicity and flexibility), events, necessity, its existing wide platform from which to build, and the demands of modern global life. There is no silver bullet as a single reason for the growth of English, but a multitude of factors working together in synergy.

In many spheres of 'demand', there is something called the 'critical mass' effect (based on the nuclear physics phenomenon of an unstoppable explosion), or sometimes called the tipping point. Broadly, it is when something like a market service, for instance, reaches such a high volume, or critical mass, that most people then want it as they feel it has become a 'must have', and being without it decreases their own standing, or status, or opportunities. In recent years we have seen this phenomena with mobile phones, the internet, flat-screen televisions, to name but three examples.

It might now be the case that we are approaching a time when there is a critical mass of English being spoken throughout the world, so people begin to feel vulnerable, or under-equipped, without this language skill, which makes it impossible to stop its growth, and will ensure its growth will accelerate even more. The possibility of this is difficult to predict, as it is unique for this to happen with a language, but the growth in English does have some of the hallmarks of approaching a critical mass.

To further underline this growth, it is now thought that about 85% of all international organisations have English as one of their official languages, and about 1/3 of international organisations use English only.

It is my strong belief that the growth of English will continue in the future, critical mass or not. Whether this is a positive thing will be discussed later in this book. However, English will continue to be used internationally around the world. Of that, there is no doubt. So, let us now examine its growth in more depth.

History of English 'Growth'

Historically, the growth of English around the world has been by evolution rather than imposition. This type of organic growth adds to its strength as natural growth is invariably tougher, and longer lasting than forced growth.

The English speakers colonising foreign lands in past centuries did not impose English upon the people they colonised. Unlike the Spanish, French, or Portuguese that did insist colonised populations spoke their language, the British did not impose their language. Wherever the Spanish went to conquer and colonise, they imposed both their religion and culture; South America being the classical example. Their religion, Christianity, which they enforced upon their new colonial subjects with absolute ruthlessness, was their most effective tool for implanting their own language and culture. Likewise, the French and Portuguese adopted very much the same approach, though with less determination than the Spanish who had their fanatically religious monarchs, notably Philip II, to enforce this policy (the same Philip that tried to invade England until Francis Drake and friends scotched that little scheme).

The English, on the other hand, did not try to impose Christianity, and English culture, and language upon their new colonial subjects. In fact, in our largest colony by far, India, and to some extent in African colonies, the English prohibited or strongly discouraged missionaries arriving and trying to convert local populations to Christianity and any imposition of English or Englishness. They preferred to live alongside native populations with their separate cultures, keeping their distance, maintaining stability and using translators where necessary. They had only one paramount aim in mind; trade, trade, and trade (the Dutch had a similar approach). In fact, huge countries like India were not colonised by the English government or crown at all, initially, but by the British East Indian Company, a merchant company in which trade was always paramount, and certainly not religious or linguistic conversion of any type.

This makes the steady and relentless rise in the spread of the English language even more interesting. There was no central authority determined to 'anglicise' colonised communities, so the desire to speak English in such places as India, for instance, has been more voluntary, or evolutionary, rather than imposed or demanded.

North America is a good example of how English incrementally became the language of choice. These great lands were first colonised by the Spanish, with their accompanying imperial rule as previously described, and Spanish speakers dominated what is now Texas, Florida, and even southern California. The French were dominant in North America's southern east coast (Louisiana), and even more so in Canada. There were also large numbers of immigrants to the US that were German speaking, Dutch speaking, and Italian speaking, and became communities embedded at different times in different places in North America, whilst the English migration was, initially, mainly focussed on the region now known as New England – a strip of the northern east coast of that vast continent – and the colonisation was not British government led, but Puritan settlers seeking a new life.

So why did English emerge as the dominant language of the vast North America continent, now known as the USA and Canada, and not Spanish, or French, or even German?

My answer is perhaps unsurprising, but the simplicity of English won the day. The basic language is easy to learn and use, as previously explained. That is why it superseded its formidable competitors of Spanish and French. It was successful not because of physical conquest, overwhelming numbers, central direction, or religion, but the simplicity and ease by which English can be learnt in its fundamental form. This simplicity was vital for the ever increasing flood of new settlers to that continent from around the world, or certainly from various European countries. These new settlers had to communicate within their newly adopted communities, and they instinctively chose the easiest language, English. These tough, independently minded settlers would not be dictated to anyway, and would choose and decide what they wanted to do, not what someone told them, and they collectively and incrementally chose English as their common language – as it was easy to learn and assimilate.

Here is a good place to introduce the concept of 'language politics' trying to distort reality by explaining a strange and interesting myth that has lingered in the USA for almost two centuries. It concerns America narrowly choosing English as their national language over the alternative of the German language. This myth has become known as the Muhlenberg legend and is quite well documented.

Frederick Muhlenberg was the first ever Speaker of the newly established US House of Representatives, and it was during his Speakership that the events giving birth to this legend occurred. In 1794 (the year before the American Revolution started), a group of Pennsylvania German immigrants asked that some laws be translated into German so they could understand them. This request was rejected by one vote in The House (which at that time was located in Pennsylvania, not Washington) and Speaker Muhlenberg was later quoted as saying that 'the faster these Germans became Americans, the better it will be.'

That should have been the end of what was really a quite local issue. But, it didn't end there. The reason this legend initially developed was due to an 1847 German visitor to the US, a man called van Loher, writing a book (in German) titled 'The History and Achievements of Germans in America'. Loher wrote that the 1794 vote was whether to accept German or English as the US national language, and this vote was narrowly defeated. Whether he mischievously distorted the facts, or not, we don't know. However, he did distort the facts and this was the start of the myth.

Suppression is frequently the nurturer of myths, and some American nationalists, towards the end of the 19th century, foolishly tried to eradicate and suppress minority languages in the US. To compound this attempt of minority suppression, during and after World War 1, the fear of immigrants and their foreign languages caused further language suppression and calls for English only to be allowed in the US.

In addition to this outburst of intolerance, the German language myth was further exploited by the Nazis in the 1930s for reasons of self-aggrandisement and propaganda. Even as late as 1987 a letter to the newspaper, The Chicago Sun-Times, urging the importance of voting in general, incorrectly referred to the Muhlenberg vote giving the United States English instead of German. Such is the power of myths and legends that, like conspiracy theories, they keep popping up like weeds and there are always people that want to believe in them. In fact, the US has no government dictated official language at all, but English has come to envelop that huge continent by its own simple strengths.

Britain also established colonies in Australia and New Zealand and, naturally, the new British colonists (some very unwilling deportees and more willing migrants) took their native English language with them. In these new world continents there was no competition for the dominance of English. There were indigenous Aborigines and Maoris with their own languages, of course, but they were low in population density for such large land masses, and no competition to the large numbers of new British settlers.

The British had the largest Empire the world has ever seen and it was widely spread around the globe, so this meant that English speaking communities were implanted, strategically, world-wide. This was the case in many parts of Africa, Asia, India, the Middle East, North America, South America (British Guyana and British Honduras), and the Caribbean. The dominance of the English language varied between these colonies, but this global spread was certainly a key factor in establishing English as a world language.

English did have serious competition, especially from the Spanish and French languages. The competition from the Spanish language was based upon the numbers and spread of Spanish colonies and, consequently, its Spanish speakers. The Spanish had also spread their colonisation net far and wide during their golden period of exploration and seemingly unlimited wealth gained from South American gold and silver. However, their global domination had ceased by the 17th and 18th century, due to their own problems in Spain.

The Portuguese language was, and still is, the main language of the South American continent, not Spanish as many believe though, unlike Spanish, Portuguese is not 'spread'. Its South American dominance is due to the high population of Portuguese speaking Brazil compared with other South American countries. So, Portuguese was never really a competitor language to English as it just did not have the spread.

The French language competition was not so much on the numbers and spread of their language, though this was considerable, but the French language had the additional advantage of being, for a long while, the official language of diplomacy. However, this linguistic advantage began to disappear with the fading fortunes, indeed disasters, of France during the 19th and 20th centuries following a string of military defeats and revolutions.

What about the Chinese language? The number of Chinese native speakers is huge, around four times as big as its nearest rivals, Spanish and English, but this is almost entirely due to the population numbers of the Chinese people in China. The Chinese were not travellers and colonists, so their vast language numbers are mainly sequestered within their own country and their nearby areas of influence in East Asia. This might change, of course, as China exerts more influence as its economy grows, and it spreads its influence more globally. But, let's be honest – how easy is it to learn Chinese?

The emergence of Britain as a major world and colonial power, and hence a potential spreader of its mother tongue, was mainly due to its dominance of the seas, and its thirst for trade. This global spread of Empire also lasted a long time, unlike other transient Empires, and certainly provided an excellent platform for the future growth of the English language.

The Present Growth of English

Having looked at the history of the growth of English language around the globe, why does English continue to grow and spread around the world in present times, and probably into the future?

I would argue very strongly that its simplicity is certainly a fundamental reason for its continuing spread. However, there have to be other driving forces to propel this spread in addition to its simplicity. Learning any new language in addition to your own requires considerable effort, no matter how easy the language may be to learn. There has to be motivation and driving forces to spend time learning something, anything, especially another language.

The reasons driving this growth, I believe, are:

Hollywood, Disney, English speaking cinema and TV
Pop music
The ex-British Empire and now Commonwealth
The American dream
The Internet and Apple
School education
China
Global communication for interlinked worldwide industries (e.g. air travel)
Globalisation of trade
Tourism
Modern careers
T-shirts and adverts

These reasons are not listed in terms of importance, or chronological occurrence. That is because I would not be able to give them any hierarchy of importance, and rather than being hierarchal, these reasons work differently in different places, depending upon factors such as age groups, occupations, type of person, type of government, and they also work in synergy: interacting, enhancing and supporting each other. What is most important is the large number of factors that exist, nudging each other along, and this magical and potent mixture of 'drivers' are all present now, together.

Take **Hollywood** and, to a lesser extent, the British Film Industry. There are many countries that make good quality films and programmes, but none with the sheer volume and universal appeal of the English speaking world. Blockbusters like Titanic, Gladiator, James Bond, Star Trek, Star Wars, Avalon, ET, Four Weddings and a Funeral, Pirates of the Caribbean, are just a few of the many hundreds of very popular films that are watched the world over. Their appeal is, to some extent, due to the investment and creativity that goes into these movies, but also the pure volume in which Hollywood is able to churn out movies with such a wide spectrum of subjects.

Some countries, notably France, Germany, Italy and Spain, use dubbing to interpose their own language over the English speaking movies but very many more countries don't use dubbing, and use sub-titles instead. Many of my own students have said that sub-titles are one of the main reasons why their English learning has improved and been helped. They listen to the movie in English, whilst translating simultaneously into their own language. It is a type of subliminal learning, certainly, but very real nonetheless.

And it is an enjoyable way to learn. The secret to effective learning is to enjoy what you are doing whilst learning, and movies provide this magical mixture.

British comedy has undoubtedly played its part, also. Whilst living abroad in Europe I was amazed at the frequency that comedy programmes like 'Allo Allo', Fawlty Towers, Blackadder, Only Fools and Horses, to name but four of many, were repeatedly shown on local television. Again, with sub-titles. Again, sub-consciously embedding the English language into the minds of watchers.

Disney was, and still is, a superb catalyst for the growth of English and deserves a special mention. I know it is part of the Hollywood factor, but it is deliberately aimed at young children, and young children absorb new language much more easily and faster than adults. I know one example to reinforce a point is dangerous, though this example I am about to describe is far from being an isolated case. I taught a young girl in ex-Yugoslavia who not only spoke excellent English when she came to me, but even her accent was mid Atlantic (she didn't really need my help, but that's ambitious parents for you!). When asked if she had lived in an English speaking country she said no, and she hadn't even visited an English speaking country. How, then, I asked her, when she had been a student for some while, had she learnt to speak such proficient, fluent English? Without a moment's hesitation she said, "Cartoons. I loved cartoons as a child, especially Disney – and that is how I mainly learnt – sitting and watching cartoons."

I also came across a couple of very young, non-native English children, role-playing a Disney cartoon and reciting passages word perfect. There are many Disney block-busters and they cross the world in popularity, spreading the exposure to English.

It is amazing, is it not? Hollywood, Pinewood and Disney may make a lot of money producing silver screen delights for our consumption, but little do they realise how much they are also spreading the English language. I doubt if the young girl I described was a genius in being able to absorb her English glued to the telly whenever the opportunity arose, and I am certain that there are many thousands of children like her, watching animated Disney type cartoons, all around the world. What better age for a person to absorb a new language?

In a more abstract but equally important way, Hollywood and its associates also project to their viewers the pleasurable, liberal, humorous, and hedonistic aspects of 'western life', which in turn provokes the desire to learn English (or should we say American?). A remarkably intelligent youth in one of my wife's English classes, who for some strange reason also knew the advert script of a well-known English supermarket, said that his country (ex-Yugoslavia) was emerging from the 'tyranny of communism'! Where he developed this view and learnt such a description, I don't know, though it seems to sum up an attitude, or way of thinking, that also benefits the spread of the English language: The English language's association with freedom, liberalism, democracy, and consumerism. It is easy to have endless discussions about the benefits and disadvantages of 'English speaking propaganda' but, undoubtedly, I believe this western lifestyle is a motivational factor to encourage the learning of English, whether you agree with the attractiveness of the western lifestyle, or not. It is in your face, and Hollywood and its cohorts project glamour and attraction, clearly labelled with the English language.

The **BBC**, and its contemporaries, Sky and CNN, have also been a factor. On many occasions I have been told by local people in East European countries, for instance, that when it comes to news, the BBC, Sky, and CNN were, and often still are, the only reliable sources of believable news, as well as being highly watchable. Again, they may also use sub-titles (with a few seconds delay, and some terrible translations) but these news channels are playing their part in the relentless spread of the English language. Good visual imagery combined with plain English is a powerful tool for spreading English, and embedding English into the minds of watchers and listeners. Across the world's airports, I have also seen many large TVs in waiting areas showing BBC and CNN rolling news, usually with sub-titles. It is easy for people such as ourselves to take for granted that the BBC, Sky, and CNN make news interesting with their powerful mixtures of outside broadcasts, glamorous studios, monitor interviews, and graphics, but you only have to see the news broadcasts of many other countries to see how boring news programmes can be, and how watchable the BBC, Sky, CNN etc. really are. Again, using English.

Then we have **pop music.** Pop giants such as Elvis, The Beatles, The Stones, Phil Collins, The Eagles, Queen, Adele, Oasis, Beyoncé and many more English language pop singers are heard and enjoyed the world over by many people (as well as providing ubiquitous and irritating *musak* in shops everywhere; I heard English pop songs used as musak in a very well-known French supermarket, in France, very recently). I have heard students sing English language pop songs almost word perfect. They may not fully understand the meanings of all the words but they can repeat them almost word perfect and with amazingly good pronunciation. Again, another small, or not so small, way to embed the English language into people's minds. Combining pleasure with learning.

The hugely popular group ABBA deserves special mention here. Their music was extremely popular and played the world over (and still is played a lot), with many of their lyrics mimicked by many listeners and across many ages of people. Their popularity has been reinforced in recent years by an extremely successful and popular movie, and continuing theatre shows. The extraordinary thing about ABBA, which is easily forgotten when listening to them, but well known, is they are Swedish, not native-English-speakers, singing in perfect English. This achievement in itself promotes the concept of non-native-English-speakers linking English to success.

I have also been told by my students that the 'sound' of the English language is 'musical' and perfect for modern music. I do not know if this is true, and claim no expertise on modern pop music, but I have often been told that our language sounds pleasant and musical to the ear.

The past **British Empire**, or now the British Commonwealth, is another powerful factor to be taken into account for helping with the spread of English. There have been many 'Empires', but none as large and widespread as the British Empire. I do not give an opinion on the merits or otherwise of this fact, but fact it is. Although I fully understand some may strongly dispute the following assertion, I firmly believe that British colonial rule was not as despised or hated as much as the colonial rule of many other European nations, and this has had a significant effect on the post-colonial relationships enjoyed by Britain with their commonwealth partners.

The decolonisation process, post-World War 2, was conducted, by and large, in a reasonably civilised way between Britain and its colonies (with some notable exceptions, I accept). The Empire legacy left behind in many ex-colonies of British administration and institutions, their links with British universities, British military training, and British legal training was, and still is, largely admired, retained, and copied by many of Britain's ex-colonies; albeit in many localised forms. This has also helped to encourage the learning of English.

The successor to the Empire was the Commonwealth, and membership of this 'club' is large, varied and voluntary, and again passively encourages a sympathy and affinity for the English language. There are presently 52 sovereign states that are members of the Commonwealth, or which the Queen of England is the Head. Their total combined population is 2.2 billion people, about a $1/3^{rd}$ of the world's population.

In recent years I had the opportunity to visit Nigeria; a very large African country, now a commonwealth member, with a burgeoning population. When I (foolishly) asked at a business meeting if the participants would be able to use English for the business proceedings, my question was greeted with considerable indignation, almost anger. Of course, was the reply, English is our official language, don't you know (I didn't know at the time). The locals (outside the meeting) spoke Pidgin English to each other that I found difficult to understand, but they could always understand me and respond to my English.

Another business visit to Singapore was an equal eye-opener. Not only was English mainly spoken by everyone I met, including shopkeepers and café staff, but all signs and adverts were mainly in English, with sub-titles in the local Chinese or Malaysian.

It is remarkable that such very different countries as the small, Asian Singapore, and very large, African Nigeria, have not adapted their own indigenous languages following de-colonisation. The logic would be to throw away the past and remnants of colonial rule, and that the English language would be one of the first casualties of post-colonisation. Surprisingly, this has not happened. Why hasn't English been rejected by these countries? Could it be that it has not been rejected because of the language's simplicity to learn and, therefore, a convenient language for these diverse communities to integrate and communicate internally; combined with a respect for British institutions; plus the obvious advantage of being able to communicate internationally?

I don't know, I am using intuitive analysis, and doubt if any deep research could absolutely determine the answer. Whatever the reasons, the outcome is beyond dispute; many nations of the commonwealth use English as their official language, and seem to do so with relish. They obviously see the advantage of having the use of a world language.

In terms of the English language being used post-colonially, there is the rather strange case of the

Philippines, a country which I have mentioned previously. The Philippines is a very large group of islands off the North Pacific Ocean, snuggled between China and Indonesia, which were colonised by Spain in the early 1500s, and presently has a growing population of about 99 million people. In the manner of the conquering Spanish, this large spread of islands were forcibly made to submit to the Spanish religion (Catholic Christianity), the Spanish language, and the group of islands were even re-named after King Philip II of Spain.

The Philippines remained a Spanish colony for over 350 years, a long time, before, very briefly, becoming an American colony in the early 20th century after a bloody conflict between the Philippines and America. The Philippines then suffered six years of Japanese occupation during the Second World War, before finally gaining its independence after the war. What is strange is that only Filipino (a Polynesian language) and English are its official languages, used for government, education, print, broadcast media, and business. Not the Spanish language, which you would expect. In fact, Spanish has declined so much it is hardly used now in those islands. There is no reason given for choosing English as an official language, in view of the preceding 350 years of Spanish colonisation compared with only a short and unhappy period of American colonisation amidst bloody conflict, but that is what the Filipinos have done. They have chosen to have English as their alternative official language. Perhaps, once again, simplicity and pragmatism have played their part in their choice of a working language that can also be used internationally?

Then there is the much more abstract '**American dream**' factor to be considered in the spread of English, already touched upon earlier in the explanation of the role of Hollywood in promoting English. It is fashionable amongst the intellectual cadre of Europe to despise 'Americanism' and their consumerism-led society (not my view, but the view of many). I think these European intellectuals are out of touch with the views of general world populations, including their own populations. Many ordinary Europeans, Asians, Africans, Arabs, and Latin Americans admire America as the land of opportunity, equality, and glamour, even if they don't always agree with their actions and foreign policy. Many love McDonalds, Levis, chewing gum, Hollywood movies, iPhones, and the many other American innovations. American culture is seen as glamorous, attractive, modern and simply more fun. Bound to this attraction comes the American language, English. For many young people it is 'cool' to speak English and imbibe some of this easy-going western culture. This opinion may be scorned by some, but methinks they scorn in blinkered ignorance and wishful thinking. This desire to live, or copy, the American dream, and understand their cool language, should not be underestimated. It is yet another very powerful motivator for wanting to use English.

Closely linked to America is the Dotcom Revolution. The **Internet** has now been widely available to many of the world's population for over two decades (since about 1995) following the invention of the World Wide Web by British computer scientist, Tim Berners-Lee. The Internet and associated systems such as Facebook, Linked-in, Facetime, Twitter, are undoubtedly associated with

America and Silicon Valley. The Internet is a low cost, world-wide conduit to communicate, interact, and gain knowledge and information throughout the world. It is true that many countries use the internet in their own language, including the use of Google, but having used 'foreign' internet sources and foreign Google, it is amazing how much these foreign language sites are peppered with the English language. Also, my students (always a valuable source of language insights) often say that, instead of using their own country's Google or portals, they prefer to use Google.com as it is 'better'. Now, I don't know if it really is 'better', and whether there is some internet snobbery going on here, and I don't report this with any judgement of my own, but simply repeat what I have been told by these non-English users on many occasions.

The Internet is undoubtedly dominated by the English speaking world and, again, this is another way in which the English language is propagated. In the last 10–15 years, this has been greatly reinforced by the Apple revolution with iPods, iPads, and iPhones, all strongly associated with America, and loved by millions.

This link with America and English may change, of course, but certainly in the early part of the 21st century, the internet and dotcom, Windows and Google, Amazon, Yahoo, Facebook, Twitter, Instagram, Apple, etc., are all very much seen as products of the English speaking world, mainly America. Again, sub-consciously, embedding the English language and user friendliness into the minds of users.

A very powerful promoter of any subject, including the English language, is **school education**. Very many countries now teach English language as either a compulsory or voluntary subject. There are two countries that, historically, did not have good English language skills; Spain and Italy. Then Italy, in the 90s, decided to make English a compulsory subject for their schools. Accompanying this was an amazing increase in Italians wanting to gain a 'prestigious' English language qualification (Cambridge and Trinity English language certificates). Now, if I am in Italy and I want information, I always seek out someone below the age of about 30 years old, knowing that I can usually converse with them in English.

More recently, Spain, even more remarkably, has joined this English learning band-wagon, albeit that Spanish is a world language in its own right. I was curious why, from about 2014, I was suddenly examining, in England, a lot of Spanish primary teachers. Very many of them were spending time in England to improve their English they told me. I finally enquired why this was, to be told that the Spanish government were insisting that certain subjects would be increasingly taught in English in their schools. This is amazing, especially as Spanish is such an international language. Perhaps it is to do with their huge tourist trade? I don't know, but that is what has happened. So, I now look for young people when I am in Spain to ask for directions and invariably have success (having said that, as I write this, travelling in mid Spain, I have recently been given excellent directions, in very good English, by two separate local bus drivers who were certainly not young, and the place I was visiting was not a tourist town!).

Then there is **China** as a very powerful and important factor when considering the accelerating use of English throughout the world in recent times. China is very important because of its relative newness to the world stage and because of its size, burgeoning economy, and increasing involvement with the world. I mark English language exam essays for a well-known International English examination organisation. Back in the late 90s there were very few essays from China to mark. Ten years later, there were so many essays from the Chinese that examination marking was divided into China and 'Rest of the World'. The numbers of Chinese doing this international certificate was, and still is, so huge it is difficult to keep up with the demand for marking and examiners! It is almost overwhelming. That increase is remarkable, and indicates how seriously the Chinese now take their need to communicate in English. It seems, in typical Chinese style, that once they decide to do something, they really go for it in a big way. They have certainly gone for it in a big way, and their standard of English is remorselessly improving, if the standard of their English examinations is used as an indicator.

Not much happens in China without the authority of the central governing party. There is official encouragement for the learning of English as witnessed by the teaching of it in all urban primary schools, probably as they see this as an important tool for their business development and exports. It has also coincided with the Chinese economic colonisation of other parts of the world, notably in Africa and parts of the Middle East. In these places English is the language used for commerce and transactions, not Chinese. According to an article in a newspaper called the China Daily, as long ago as 2010, approximately $1/3^{rd}$ of the population of China is learning English.

A similar explosion in English language learning has happened in South Korea. The South Korean population is much smaller than China's – 20 times smaller – but their world-wide business expansion and penetration in many types of commerce is formidable, and probably this is the driving force behind their very notable increase in English speaking.

Then there is the use of English for global communication in those **interlinked world-wide industries** where world-wide communication is absolutely essential, such as in air travel. English has long being the official operating language of the air travel and maritime industries. Probably less well known is that English is also now the dominant language of international banking.

In areas such as flying, it is obvious why an international language is necessary; it is needed to request and receive understandable instructions and information between all concerned when flying all over the world. This requirement also applies in the international maritime industry and most maritime officers have a competent level of English to be able to do their job. In business, which is increasingly globalised, English is now considered to be almost obligatory in order to obtain professional or management type positions. Students know this, and so, for non-English speaking students that are ambitious, English is becoming almost a mandatory **career skill** to have.

Some years ago I was asked by an ex-student how he could obtain a copy of his English Language certificate awarded for English intermediate level, as he had lost it.

He was an engineer. Of course I obliged and obtained a copy, but I asked him why it was so important, and he told me that he was applying for a job with Siemens, the German engineering giant, and they required their professional and management staff to have this certificate of English competence. These days, to many students in non-English speaking countries, having an English qualification and proof of competent English is not just a 'nice to have' certificate, it is considered a career essential.

Conferences are another place where, usually, a knowledge of English is a must. I have attended conferences in Asia and the Middle East in recent years, usually at 'conference centres'. In wandering around the different conferences for a break from my own, it is remarkable just how many of the wide range of conference subjects are held in English in foreign lands.

Globalisation of trade is not just a political or business concept, it is a reality that is increasing and deepening remorselessly. In banking, air travel, shipping, electronics, pharmaceuticals, defence, fashion and clothing, food, cars, and for many other goods, the demand for trade, for negotiation, for deal making, for information exchange, for exchange of goods, is now world-wide and this demand requires effective communications, and that is increasingly being achieved by using English. This may only be a small paragraph explaining globalisation as a 'driver' of the English language, but the importance of world-wide trade needing a world-wide language is an extremely strong force.

Tourism is an industry that has increased dramatically in the last 50 years or so. When I say tourism, I mean foreign tourism, which means people going from their home country to a foreign country for holidays, adventure, and interest. The enormous rise in tourism in the past 50 years has meant that many people of different nationalities and different languages, have travelled to distant places and are often thrown together with many other nationalities in these favoured locations for tourists. So, in many of these places where tourists from all over the world are gathering, their hosts have to provide the many aspects of tourism needs and demands, for the enjoyment of their guests. How do they communicate with this multi-lingual group of guests? The answer is by using English. This use of English in multi-national tourist resorts is now very noticeable. The guides, hotel staff, shop keepers, and the many other persons involved in dealing with tourist foreign guests cannot possibly be expected to communicate in 5, 10, 20 different languages, so they have resorted to using English as the lingua franca. I have talked to tourism staff about this and been told that it is almost impossible to now have a key role in the tourist business without a working knowledge of English.

So far, I have been describing what I think are the big main 'drivers' (driving forces) for the spread of English and many of these reasons are probably obvious, noticeable, and beyond dispute. I have simply pointed them out and brought them together in one chapter of this book. Some of these driving factors are less obvious, though very visible, but less noticeable in a strange way, and they do make a difference in spreading the use of English and embedding it into people's minds. Two such more subtle driving forces are T-shirts and adverts.

I have been lucky enough to travel widely, and not so long ago I became aware of the **T-shirt** phenomena, though it had been around for some time before it entered my consciousness. It is amazing how many people in non-English speaking countries now wear T-shirts (or 'tops' as women might prefer) with English words splattered across their chests, full in our faces. It can be one or two words, or several words and phrases or sayings, some using benign language, some humorous language, some outrageous language, some incomprehensible language, some very meaningful, some meaningless; but it is another area where the use of English seems to dominate.

I do not know why this has happened. Perhaps it is driven by the desire of the wearer to appear 'international', or clever, or fashionable; who knows. Whatever the reason, it has happened and has been happening for quite a long time now, even though we may not have noticed. It may seem almost trite to point out this phenomena, but surely this is another indicator that English is now taken for granted as a global language, and such use of English maintains that drip feed of acceptance into people's minds. To many, it is cool.

This subtle drip feed also happens in **adverts** in non-English speaking countries. Not to the same extent as the T-shirt phenomena I have described, but quite often I see advert posters or TV adverts in these countries, and within such adverts will often be an English word or phrase, seemingly without rhyme or reason. I say without rhyme or reason possibly because I cannot understand the rest of the advert, though in reality, marketing people are usually very clever at their job and they do this, I imagine, to catch the eye, or appear international, or for some strong commercial reason. They do it, for whatever reason, because it works. And, again, this adds to the subliminal embedding of the English language into the minds of non-English speakers.

I have been describing the driving factors which I think push along the growth in English as the international language. The factors are many: Hollywood, English language news, America, the Commonwealth, globalisation, advertising, the Internet, business and commerce, English language education, tourism, even T-shirts. And, these factors, big and small, are acting together in synergy of coincidence. This bombardment of the English language into people's consciousness, combined with the simplicity of basic English, are the reasons, I believe, for the increasing spread and use of English.

It is a very powerful combination of driving forces and motivators coming together and, almost by accident, reinforcing each other. It is a combination without any central authority, without any orchestration or regulation, and that is precisely the sort of environment in which English thrives and probably what makes it even more formidable.

12. Will English Continue to Grow?

Guessing what this world's diverse human population will do in the future is highly inadvisable because of its unpredictability. What we can do is look at the past, the present, and on-going trends to try and predict probabilities for the future.

The conditions for the continued growth of English as an international language seem almost perfect as things stand. The English language is not a new fashion, come one day and gone another. It has been in existence for many centuries, growing steadily, and has strength tempered with simplicity, resilience and flexibility. Summarising:

- English has had a worldwide presence for a long time, so it is an accepted fact
- It has a history of seeing-off competitors, such as witnessed in America and the Philippines
- The language is adaptable to local conditions, and is free to evolve and adapt without any regulatory interference
- It is 'learner friendly' because of its simplicity

- Accelerating globalisation of commerce, travel, fashion, food, news, and telecommunications requires world-wide communication, and English is readily available to fill that need
- English has powerful 'drivers' and catalysts, such as America, the Commonwealth, Hollywood, globalisation, and the Internet to continue to support its spread.

So, English is in an ideal position to increasingly become the international language of the world, and I see no competitor language with anything approaching the present advantages of English.

How fast will the spread of the English language continue? My belief is that its spread is accelerating, as witnessed in China and Korea, and their massive increase in English students and exams, for instance, and will continue to accelerate as more and more people and governments realise that they need an international language to succeed in this increasingly globalised world. Countries such as Spain, China, and South Korea are showing the way forward for countries that historically were not strong in learning English. Two countries that have world languages of their own, China and Spain, could easily adopt an attitude of disdain for this American-driven language usurper, or language relic of a past Empire, but instead they have chosen to do the opposite, and actively encourage learning English within their own countries as a practical way to improve successful opportunities for their own country. That is quite something, and demonstrates an open minded and practical attitude that is refreshing, and probably indicates the direction for other countries.

Russia (no lover of the English speaking world) has said that to become a civil servant fluent English will be required. Thailand aims to teach English to 14 million students in its state schools. In Vietnam, English is compulsory from the 4th grade (around 9–10 years old). South Sudan, with its recent history of terrible civil war and atrocities, has adopted English as its national language of unity. English does not seem to be deterred by history, prejudice, and national boundaries.

Having made my own prediction that English is going to continue to spread even wider, and is probably accelerating, I also think this will still take many years before it becomes truly global. Having said that I don't think it will happen quickly – who knows? What is quickly? When I examine the progress of the past 25 years, such as the birth of the internet, mobile phone and digital communication, and the decision of places like China to embrace English learning, it could happen more quickly. The future is highly unpredictable.

The interesting question is, though, do we really need a global language? My unequivocal answer is yes, we certainly do need a global language for communication. Globalisation of commerce, business, air travel, fashion, food, etc. is not going to decline, but increase, despite the wishes of some. There will be resistance to globalisation of production and trade, as we have already seen, with threats of trade protectionism, trade barriers, and even trade wars. Railing against change, sometimes understandably, was always present, and this type of resistance to change rears its head periodically, and has done so throughout the world's history because many people feel threatened by change, especially fast change. However, the clock cannot be turned back, despite occasional setbacks, and globalisation will undoubtedly continue, as it is unstoppable. The conundrum is that often, the people that feel most threatened by globalisation, also want cheaper products and more of them, and want to share the advantages that other nations are perceived to have. People want to travel, and learn, and that is not going to change, despite the wish for short term gains by using barriers like trade protection. This remorseless and unstoppable move to greater globalisation will underpin and reinforce the need for global communication. And this can only be effectively achieved by having an international language.

I don't know how long the expansion of English around the globe will continue, but I am certain it will, and believe it should be embraced, not resisted. I will now try to explain why a world language should be welcomed, and deal with areas of concerns such as national identity and culture, and explain why a common language amongst people should be encouraged, not deterred, and how that can only benefit us all.

13. The USA and European Union; Does Language Unite People?

In this chapter we will look at three 'Unions' of people. One of these unions is mono-lingual (speak the same language), and the other two unions are multi-lingual (speak different languages). First we will look at Europe as an example of a multi-lingual community, and the USA as a mono-lingual community. The third example will be described later.

The European Union presently has 28 member countries (UK still included at time of writing), and a population of approximately 500 million people. Whatever you think of Europe as an entity, or the existing European Union as a political union, trading union, or customs union, there is no doubt that it is imperative for peace in the continent of Europe that individual countries use every means they can to work together, cooperate, and endeavour to live in peace. If they don't, there is the frequently repeated and very real danger of dramatic conflict, as the past has all too often shown with miserable, devastating and tragic consequences, not just for the European countries concerned, but frequently for the world. It is in everybody's interest that the countries of

123

Europe are united in some way, and don't become disunited and opposed.

Whether the peaceful coexistence of European nations is best achieved within a pact like the existing European Union, or something similar, is not for question here, and at present the European Union is a reality with the stated aim in its treaty of *'Ever closer union of the peoples of Europe'*. So, there is no doubt that union is an aim of the partner countries of the European Union.

The European Union has a relatively stable population of 500 million people (stable in terms of birth-rates), of similar ethnicity, living in 27–28 countries, sharing the same continent; but it also recognises and uses 24 languages. The EU has its own parliament and elected members, its own president, its own court, its own flag, its own administrative centre, its own police arrest warrant, its own stirring national anthem, and most member countries presently share the same currency, the Euro. It even postures the idea of a single European defence force.

The European Union can be fairly compared with that other large union of 'the west', the United States of America. Both have fairly comparable economies in size, and both consider themselves, by and large, to be 'western civilisations', with similar political and social proclivities, aspirations and values.

The USA has a fast growing population of approximately 320 million people, with a wide variety of ethnic origins within the population, living within 50 different states sharing the same continent (with the exception of Hawaii), in a continental landmass larger than the European Union, with each US state having a high degree of legislative freedom. The USA also has its own president, its own parliament (called Congress), its own courts, its own flag, its own currency, its own federal administrative centre, and its own national anthem.

So, we have two, not dis-similar unions in terms of population, wealth, values, and ethnicity, both having administration centres but with devolved, or federal legislatures, both using the classic symbols of national unity: President, flag, currency, anthem, elected parliaments; both having a 'unite' word in their title, but, I would suggest, they are seen to have very different degrees of success in being considered as a united entity and actually managing to unite their populations. The USA has been extremely successful in uniting its people into a single entity, into a nation, but the European Union appears to be the antithesis of the USA, and not approaching any sign of being 'one entity', except perhaps in the wishful thinking of some politicians. To most people the European Union does not feel like a single cohesive entity, frequently feels as if it is about to fracture, and has administrative centres that appear detached and remote from their populations.

One of the key differences the USA does have from the European Union is that it shares one single language. The vast majority of people would agree the USA is undoubtedly one country, one nation, with a very clear and powerful identity, and the majority of its population openly love their country and share strong loyalty, and belief in their beloved constitution. They want to be united, and they clearly are. The EU say they want to be 'united', but are clearly not. In fact, there are ever increasing signs that some countries of the EU want to leave, or have a significant proportion of their population that want to leave the union.

This was also once the case with the USA. The southern states of the US wanted separation and did not want to be in the federation of a United States, and they had a particularly bloody civil war over the issue. Fortunately, the wounds healed, quickly in most respects, and splintering of the United States is never an issue nowadays.

The USA has the advantage over the EU of having been united for about 150 years if you take the end of the American civil war as the start of a true United States. Conversely, the present European Union has existed for about 60 years compared with the USA's 150 years. It could also be strongly argued that, after the utter devastation of the Second World War, Europe was so torn apart that its motivation to work closely, to re-build, and become a 'union' to avoid such a catastrophe occurring again, was very powerful. In fact the founding countries of the EU did seem to be powerfully motivated and determined to be ever closer as a union, and indeed its declared aims are *ever closer union of the peoples of Europe*. So, why does Europe seem forever bogged down in endless problems and disagreements and rarely appears to be a closely bonded union?

It is true that in the EU its separate sovereign states, unelected president, a parliament that feels estranged and distant, and a wide spectrum of political parties within the different sovereign states, all help to deter a feeling of unity. However, you also hear American citizens complain of the Washington elite that are distant from their own views, and they also have a wide spectrum of political views within their two mainstream parties.

What role does the language differences within and between the two unions play? Are the language differences in the EU under-estimated as a barrier to unity? I am convinced they are, and this language question is suppressed and rarely, if ever, discussed. The European Union has 24 official languages to cope with, compared with the single language of the USA. All these languages are officially 'respected' within the EU, and discussions between administration members are translated into each of these languages. This is a massive task. You do not have to be a mathematician to realise that translating all important discussions, and debates, and documents into these 24 different languages is a mammoth task.

It is not the financial cost of endless translations that really matters, considerable though it is and will be dealt with separately, but the lack of continuity and fluidity of language, of discussion, and of communication that is the main disadvantage of not sharing a common language. The understanding, or misunderstanding, of language differences that exist, over-layered with the obtuse language of politics, diplomacy and innuendo, are very important. The use of different languages and consequent multi-translations does not lend itself to fluidity, ready comprehension, and mutual understanding between members; and heaven knows how much is misunderstood, and even accidentally twisted during interpretation. Negotiation is of paramount importance in any union and often very demanding at times. It is exceedingly difficult to negotiate in 24 different languages, and I believe the European Union demonstrates this very clearly.

This is where the USA has a massive advantage in speaking one language. Anyone who knows America will also know that it is far from a homogenous community, and there are large cultural differences between north and south, east and west, and the white, non-white, and Hispanic populations. Arizona state (south west) and Maine state (north east) are almost 3000 miles apart (about the same distance as between Paris and Baghdad) and seem like different countries in climate, landscape, industry and some other respects. Nevertheless, the huge advantage of sharing the same language, English, enables the feeling of one entity, one nation, especially in such a large and diverse geographical area, and enables much better communication, comprehension, and easier social discourse. Internal differences that exist politically and socially can be much more readily understood, discussed and negotiated (even if they are not always solved). Communicating in the same language, within any community, is critical for social cohesiveness, identity, and bonding, regardless of the size of that community.

America is a very good example of how effectively a common language can synthesise unity between people. Consider the sheer size of the USA as a country – larger than the area of the European Union with a much more diverse environment and landscape. It has the diversity and numbers of its original immigrant settlers speaking many different languages, who poured into and settled within America over a relatively short period of time. Then it had the terrible civil war that the USA endured (often called the first modern war); plus its history of slavery and high racial tensions and bigotry that existed not that long ago. When you think of all these barriers to unity, it is almost miraculous that such a united and dynamic nation has been created in quite a short time, rather than three or four separate nations that it could have become.

The acceptance of one language amongst such a widely spread and diverse people as the USA was an extremely powerful factor in creating the feeling of one nation. It is this very powerful ingredient of one language that the European Union does not possess, and has to cope with 24 different languages. The contrast between the amount of unity of these two unions is quite startling when measured by the perspective of being part of one entity. There seems to be no competition at all in the unity stakes. The USA wins hands down.

Another other 'Union' that is interesting to compare with the EU and USA when exploring the question of unity is the now defunct Soviet Union. As the years pass since its disintegration in 1987, it seems like a distant memory; and indeed it is. During its dominance, it was a very real and terrifying opponent of the west, and seemed utterly united in its political aims and social values. That is, until it crumbled and disintegrated almost unexpectedly, within a very short period of time, and its actual lack of unity and internal antagonisms were exposed for the world to see.

The Soviet Union lasted for 70 years, and during this time its member states suffered terribly during the Second World War from a Nazi fascist force totally opposed to its values of socialism. The Soviet Union had 15 member countries, many of them of Slavic ethnicity, with a total population of about 290 million people. Its geography was contained within the largest land mass in the world, and it had an identical Soviet style of government throughout its member states, with accompanying iron rule from the centre. It had a combined, powerful army, a soviet flag, and a Soviet Union national anthem.

But, it also had many languages within its union. In addition to language differences, some used Cyrillic script, and others used Latin style script. It tried to impose Russian as a common language, but failed hopelessly in this aim, even though the many Slavic languages share some similarities. So, here is another union, with a powerful set of shared values, very strong and powerful government, the majority sharing Slavic ethnicity, but nevertheless failing hopelessly as a Union in the end. It can be argued, and it is argued, that the Soviet Union failed for many reasons; but you never hear language mentioned as a reason or a contributing factor. Is the obvious being overlooked?

Would it be different if the European Union shared a common language? Would the people of the European Union begin to feel more unified? Would one international world language be able to greatly help bind the world community much closer together? These are highly provocative questions that almost dare not be voiced in this world where separate identities and cultures are highly respected.

Perhaps it is time that such suggestions are more openly voiced, and the idea of national cultures be questioned more? Indeed, in 2013, the President of Germany, Joachim Gauck, called for English to be made the language of the European Union because, he said, inadequate communication is needed to build a more integrated European community. He argued that Europe needed a common language to encourage a sense of community.

Are these different European cultures, which include language, respected too much in this day and age? I personally think this respect for other 'cultures' and national identities, whilst being well intended, can be superficial, misguided, selective, patronising, and unrealistic for our global future. Yes, of course we should respect national sovereignty and nation states, but perhaps we need to be less sensitive to so-called national cultures, and challenge some of the myths surrounding culture, especially when such attitudes could be barriers to mutual understanding and unity of cooperation in the world.

14. Language, Culture and Identity

'Culture' is a much used word of present times and seems to be obligatory to indicate a person's or government's sensitivity and tolerance to a wide variety of habits, customs, practices and behaviours. One frequently hears phrases like, 'we must respect other peoples' cultures'. It seems to be thrown into most speeches and debates, like salt is thrown into cooking.

But, what is really meant by culture? Culture can easily be confused with identity, which is usually a simpler concept (identity = *the fact of being who or what a person or thing is)*. The Oxford English Dictionary defines culture as meaning *the customs, ideas, and social behaviour of a particular people or group.* I have heard this definition simplified even further to, '*the way we do things round here*'.

So, what determines a nation's culture – the way a nation 'does things' – that differentiates it from other nations? The reality is that it is a mixture of many things, and many of these things change.

First, it is a nation's history that mostly affects the way people of a nation do things. History includes a nation's twists and turns, the migrations and genetic mingling it has experienced, its past feuds and battles, the types of leaders the nation has had, the religious influences upon the country, and its political evolvement. History, as recorded or perceived, is not always 'true' of course, but can be subjective and even falsified. What really matters to the present day population of a nation, or region, is their past as they interpret it.

Second, a factor as basic as climate has a considerable influence on culture. We generally understand what is meant, for instance, by a Mediterranean culture. Or, the effect of the ever changing British weather on the British temperament. Living in the searing heat of the Middle East and Saharan Africa, or the bone chilling cold of Alaska and the Arctic circle, affects the way a people, or nation, 'do things', and is a strong consideration in helping to create a nation's culture.

Thirdly, a nation's landscape and soil fertility must affect the way people do things. It affects how easily they can travel, meet their neighbours, grow crops, raise livestock and, along with climate landscape and soil fertility, affect the way people live. An arid mountain country is bound to differently affect how people act in comparison with people that live in a fertile plain.

Usually, a combination of the 2nd and 3rd factors described above, climate and landscape, will also affect things like dress that later become national costumes (which is more about identity than culture). It will affect the configuration of homesteads and how people live. For instance, compare the difference between hunting from igloos compared with wandering the desert as nomads living from tents – two extreme examples of how climate and landscape affect culture – the way people 'do' things.

These three factors of history, climate, and landscape, I think set the basic foundations for a nation's culture – *the customs, ideas, and social behaviour of a particular people or group*. And then, in addition to these 'natural' determiners of culture, people develop, usually over a long period of time, a range of religious beliefs and views based on experience and leadership, and create festivities and celebrations that further add to their identity or 'culture' (the Orange marches of Ulster, and Bullfights of Spain, are two examples).

Finally, nations use symbols to identify themselves as one nation. Examples are flags, currencies, national anthems, national costumes, national celebrations, and monuments. I would argue that these symbols are all about national identity, not culture, and many tend to be quite superficial in reality. For instance, the franc would have been considered an essential part of French identity some years ago, and the lira very Italian, and likewise the deutschmark, peseta, and drachma for Germany, Spain, and Greece. That said, the adoption of one shared currency, the euro, seems to have had no impact at all upon the 'cultures' or identities of the countries concerned (notwithstanding economic considerations).

What you will have noticed is that I have not yet mentioned language as a factor in determining a country's culture or identity. Nonetheless, a country's language is often given as an example of being a very important part of a country's identity and culture, as if the French language makes the French, French. Or the German language makes the Germans, German; or the Spanish language makes the Spanish, Spanish, for instance.

I seriously challenge this view, and would question if language makes much, if any, difference to a nation's culture or identity. I think this opinion is a result of lazy analysis. What I mean is that the opinion has not been properly thought through, analysed from real evidence, and challenged. It is just assumed to be correct, as it is so often repeated, so it must be true.

To challenge this view that language is an important element of culture and identity, let us examine the evidence. I am sure a Spanish speaking Mexican would be very offended if you said they had the same, or very similar culture or identity, to Spanish speaking Argentinians. Likewise, I'm sure Chileans would consider themselves very different to Venezuelans, and Cubans would certainly not want to be compared with the country of Spain. Or, taking the Portuguese, what culture or identity do the people of Portuguese speaking Mozambique share with Portuguese speaking Brazilians, and what do either of these countries have in common with the culture of Portugal?

Even more sensitively, try telling a French speaking Belgian that they have the same or similar culture, or identity to the French. Or, telling the German speaking Austrians that they are just like the Germans. I am sure you would receive a very interesting reaction.

The same applies to the English speaking world. The Scots certainly would not claim to share the same culture as the Welsh, and just try comparing an Australian to the English. And, very sensitively, the Canadians certainly feel as if they have a very different culture and identity to their powerful USA neighbour. My point is, that language plays an insignificant role in a country's culture or identity.

It indicates, perhaps, an historical evolution, or past relationship of some sort, but that is about all.

Still not convinced? Well, let us take a look at Switzerland as a further example. Switzerland is one of the oldest Republics in the world and also has a very strong, individual culture and identity that has survived for about 700 years. It has a very distinctive history of fighting for its freedom and independence (embodied in William Tell), a history of political neutrality, religious tolerance, and is known world-wide for its yodelling, skiing, chocolate, cheese, watch-making, cuckoo-clocks, banking, the Swiss Army knife, the Geneva Convention, and its very distinctive flag. It also has the honour of being the official guard of the Vatican (the Swiss Guard) in its distinctive costumes.

But, here is the strange thing – it has four official and actually spoken languages: German, French, Italian, and Romansch. I have worked in Switzerland and met many Swiss people, and they are very loyal and proud of their country (and speak good English). If one believes that language is an important part of national identity and a cultural imperative, how do we explain the strong identity and culture of Switzerland with such language diversity?

Interestingly, English is the language used mostly by many Swiss to communicate internally between people from different language parts of their nation, if they don't understand their fellow countryman's native language.

My conclusion is that I don't really see any evidence that language is an important national identifier. It is believed it is by many, but this belief is mainly based on sentimentality, not evidence, and has never really been challenged. Sometimes, love of the language engages with this natural sentimentality. Of course the Italian and French language are interesting to hear in the opinion of many (including myself), and naturally, the language of those countries is associated with their people. However, this is different to meaning it is a national identifier. I have Italian and French friends who speak excellent English, but they don't appear any less Italian or less French when they are speaking English; they are simply more comprehensible to me.

This conclusion, that language is a poor national identifier or cultural determiner, may seem to run counter to my previous assertion that language is a great 'binder' or glue between people of one society (see mono-lingual communities), but these two assertions are not antagonistic to each other, and both can be correct.

A shared language does obviously enable people to readily communicate and therefore, hopefully, understand each other better. Even so, a shared language does not give a nation an individual identity or culture to differentiate it from other nations, even though people often like to think it does or, more importantly, are manipulated to believe it does by politicians.

Politics is more about perceptions than realities and it has often suited people, at different times, to use language as one means of differentiating, or dis-uniting, or distancing themselves from cousin nations, near neighbours, or not so near nations. In other words, instead of using language constructively, or positively, to communicate and understand each other and develop closer relationships, it can be used as a tool to be negative in relationships, and make communication and understanding more difficult.

Language was created to communicate with others, and I would suggest that using language as a tool to make communication more difficult is not a 'use' of language, rather it is an abuse. But it happens. Fortunately, it is usually unsuccessful.

15. Language and Politics

The use of language to deliberately differentiate a region from a near neighbour is not uncommon. Examples in Western Europe can be readily found in the Basque regions of Spain and France, in Wales, in Catalan, and in some remoter parts of Scotland, for instance. This political use of language is not just confined to these examples in Europe and occurs in different parts of the world.

In those areas quoted as examples above, the people seem to cling onto an ancient language as a means of trying to signal they are different from their governing big brother, or powerful neighbour. They are often comparatively small regions that are part of a larger, more dominant union, and it seems to be a way of signalling either resistance against homogenising their smaller 'culture' into that of their dominant country, or even a way to indicate their wish for independence.

I have no wish to comment upon whether such regions deserve autonomy or independence, or not. However, I do question the motivation and wisdom of using a different language to try and distance themselves, or differentiate their 'culture', from others. Language is meant to be a way of communicating with others and, by communicating, being able to explain and negotiate. Using language barriers often seem to have the opposite effect of causing a lack of understanding, and even causing resentment against the language separatists. This, in turn, can lead to more aggressive ways of the smaller region expressing their discontent, leading sometimes to extreme measures. The use of language barriers, and later the use of aggression, is usually the action of a vociferous minority, but it is the vociferous minority that often get heard the most.

Scotland is a positive and good example of how to get results by using the same language as the rest of the union it belongs to, and not trying to promote a different language. Scotland has long wanted more autonomy and recognition, and even independence, but has steadfastly stated its case in the language of the United Kingdom, English, and has successfully gained considerable autonomy and recognition. As well as using democratic politics, it has communicated its case coherently and in a language that everybody understands.

Modern democratic governments in 'the West' are tolerant of regional languages and spend money on language education, public signs, and want to appear to encourage these separate languages. It does seem to be more of a way for governments to avoid the underlying issue of dealing with the wish for local autonomy and discussing it sensibly, and understanding that government centralisation and distance can cause resentment amongst subordinate communities. Language is highly visible, especially in written form, and is a conveniently visible way of saying 'we are different around here'. In reality, I think it just causes some confusion with visitors and neighbouring communities, and does not lead to a more harmonious integrated society, which would be a much more worthwhile goal. Language apartheid does not seem to be a sensible way of communicating with neighbours, contemporaries, and the people with whom communities have to deal with and negotiate. The wisdom (and success) of the Scots is probably an example for others to follow.

This language politics can be taken to rather more extreme and incomprehensible measures. Before the terrible civil war of Yugoslavia in the 1990s, Croatia and Serbia shared a language called 'Serbo-Croat' during their one nation integrated years. Following their civil war and the break-up of Yugoslavia into smaller countries in the 1990s, one of the newly independent countries, Croatia, introduced new words into their language to try and create the separate language of 'Croatian' and differentiate it from their neighbour, Serbia. Why they wanted to do this is fairly incomprehensible as the Croatian culture and identity is very distinct and different to the Serbian culture. They did it, nevertheless. They even changed the names of the months, which people found really strange. This is a form of negative nationalism. I happened to be living there at the time this was happening, and speaking to everyday people about the 'new' words being created usually prompted head shaking (with disbelief), or even laughter, at the government's attempts to create a new language (the government at that time was particularly nationalistic and unpleasant, and were driving Serbian residents from Croatia by any means they could). It was a stark lesson to me that language could be used as a political tool in a very negative way; and certainly to discourage communication and social integration.

A more flippant example of using language in a benign but nationalistic way that I also experienced was in

Slovenia. There are words that are international and used world-wide as instantly recognisable descriptors of well-known commodities. One example is 'pizza' and 'pizzeria'. I have seen this convenience food advertised all over the world using those very words, even in Asian countries. Slovenia is a very small country that was always the underdog within the old Yugoslavia, and was the first Yugoslavian country to claim its independence (and, arguably, triggered the civil war). It is very proud of its relatively new independence. It has a distinct identity and culture of its own and, interestingly, its own language. When I say its own language, it does share very much of its language with its large neighbours, Croatia and Serbia, but it also has linguistic differences of which it is very proud. It also wants to encourage tourists to Slovenia, as it needs the revenue. However, just over the border from neighbouring Austria, which is a good source and conduit of visitors and tourists, is a large roadside restaurant that was signposted as a Pizzeria. Then, suddenly, it re-named itself as a Picerija. This new, Slovenian-style spelling, sounds the same as Pizzeria (in pronunciation), but I imagine most tourists would not have a clue what 'Picerija' means, and would probably drive past in ignorance. How self-defeating is that for the restaurant owner? It is a benign and frivolous example of the politics of language, and it does have its roots in a mild form of nationalism, self-defeating though it may be.

Of course, there are also examples of language being used more positively. America can be seen as an example of deciding to use one language, English, to help bind a huge, diverse, and widely spread country together as one nation.

Probably a less well known, but important language change, was the decision, in 1928, by the enigmatic Turkish leader, Ataturk, to successfully change the Turkish alphabet to Latin script instead of the previous Arabic script which it had used for centuries. The aim was to encourage a more western outlook and social culture for the future amongst its people. Considering the previous very significant power of the Turkish Ottoman Empire, and the many conflicts in which this Empire had been involved against the west, this was using language as a political tool and, from a western perspective, a very positive use of this tool.

So, language manipulation can be used, and is used, politically, for both positive and negative reasons. It can be a powerfully positive tool if used cleverly, but does not really seem to achieve much when used negatively, nationalistically, or parochially; except to alienate communities and reduce communication.

16. Costs of Language Diversity

It was when living in Slovenia, ex-Yugoslavia, that I first became aware of the financial cost of a language, something that had never crossed my mind before.

Despite the much lower cost of living in Slovenia at that time compared with west European countries such as England and France, books were surprisingly expensive. There were a few reasons for this, but one very significant reason was that non-Slovenian books, which were many of the books, as Slovenia is a very small country, had to be translated from their original language into Slovenian. And this adds a significant cost to the price of a book.

I also realised that the use of sub-titles for non-Slovenian television and movies must also have a financial cost which has to be passed on, somehow, to consumers or providers. Someone has to pay for the creation and insertion of sub-titles, as they do the translation of books.

This then started to make me think about the financial cost of language, which I had never before considered. When I started to enquire more about this cost, I came against a wall of silence and a vacuum of information. It was not a conspiratorial wall of silence, but there was simply no research on the subject of collective translation costs, and nobody had even thought about the subject, as far as I could find out. So, you are left wondering whether the cost of translating a huge amount of information and data, coming in and going out of a country, is to be measured in thousands of euros, or millions of euros each year? I could not find the answer and I still don't know the cost to that one country of all the translation that is necessary for user manuals, books, movies, government papers, records, websites; but I am sure it is considerable.

The break-up of former Yugoslavia, of which Slovenia was a part, was a good illustration of both the politics of language and the cost of language. One country, Yugoslavia, had fragmented into several new countries: Slovenia, Croatia, Serbia, Bosnia, Montenegro, Macedonia, and Kosovo. And, from having one dominant language used throughout Yugoslavia, Serbo-Croat, which had been understood by the general population, and used in schools and government, there were now five languages that all required cross translations and interpretation. This language fragmentation must, therefore, have a very significant cost, but a significant cost that certainly isn't recorded, or even discussed. I doubt if the general population even think about its costs.

I was closely involved in one particular commercial undertaking – to organise the translation of detailed operating manuals for an international car-seat production company that required its English working manuals (from America) to be translated into the local language for use in that country. There were dozens of manuals, and many of the instructions were highly technical, involving engineering vocabulary. Checking for correct translation with the operators that were dealing with the manufacture and fitting of the seats was a costly and very time consuming task, and was on-going as new car seats were constantly being made. It was very expensive for the parent company and, once again, that cost had to be paid for by someone. This is just one example of the cost of separate languages, but I am sure many more such undertakings exist in many other countries. It is a cost that is not centrally recorded or monitored, but a cost nevertheless. And this process will go on in many countries for many different reasons.

I then turned to the European Union for cost information of languages, as the EU has a massive translation and interpretation service. It has 24 officially recognised languages which it has to accommodate. Like many costs in the European Union, transparency is not the strong point of that institution and it is very difficult to find out the costs of very much, least of all the cost of their present translation and interpretation service.

The European Parliament does give some figures on their website, albeit many years out of date, about the costs of this giant translation task. Here is a summary of some of its statements on their website (note the years quoted):

- For 2006, the translation cost in all EU institutions is estimated at €800 million.
- Multilingualism expenditure represents over $1/3^{rd}$ of the total expenditure of Parliament.
- The European Parliament translated 673,000 pages during the first half of 2007.
- Since 2005, the European Parliament has translated over a million pages a year.

- The EU system on average requires over 2000 translators and 800 interpreters per day.

These figures are very clearly dated (11 years out of date at the time of this writing in 2017), but are the only figures they make available, and since 2006, three other countries have joined the EU, each with their own languages: Romania, Bulgaria, and Croatia. Considering it is over 11 years since that figure of €800 million was published, and three new members have since joined, and the administration of the EU has increased, I would think that a reasonable estimate of the translation costs now (2017) could be as much as €1.2 billion per year. That is €1,200,000,000 per year. Or over a decade €12,000,000,000; which is twelve thousand million euros.

Twelve thousand million euros. That is a lot of money, and it is certainly not insignificant. A lot could be done with 1200 million euros each year within the EU, I'm sure. And, this cost is not investment money to improve roads, or develop regions, or help industries, or improve farming, or provide housing, or help refugees, or create a defence capability; it is money spent on a form of administration that is non-productive, translation, and even slows down the administrative processes.

Now, I can understand how a disinterested onlooker may think that it is entirely reasonable for the European Union to take all member languages into consideration, however small an individual member country may be, but I doubt if many people ever think of its cost vs. benefit. It is certainly a very significant cost.

Another institution that has a very big translation and interpretation cost is the United Nations. It has six working languages which are Arabic, Chinese, English, French, Russian, and Spanish. Interestingly, it has drawn criticism in recent years for relying too heavily on English. I suspect the natural growth of English is seen as a more convenient way of communicating day to day, as many members will use and understand English but, as ever, the politics of language is being used as a barrier against unity, which is a bit rich for a United Nations!

Using different languages does have a cost, and a very significant cost. It is a cost that is not really talked about, discussed, even recognised. It is not a centralised cost, with the exception of the European Union and the United Nations, so it is almost impossible to estimate what is the total cost of using different languages and translations world-wide. However, from the example of the European Union described above, it is a very significant amount of money and expertise to be diverted from other forms of human development.

17. Brain Space – How Many Languages Can You Learn Anyway?

A normal human being can only learn so much, and that learning is limited by a person's brain capacity and time.

How do you learn? You can learn cognitively (naturally) by observation and experience over a period of time, such as very young children learn to walk, talk, toilet, socialise, dress, and so on. Or you can learn by being taught (including self-teaching), which requires effort, concentration, and dedicated time.

Opinions vary on how the brain operates, and its capacity to assimilate and learn, and some believe that the brain can assimilate much more than we require of it normally. There are undoubtedly gifted people in the world that can assimilate a lot of knowledge or expertise in particular subject areas, or learn music or languages much faster, or more easily than the general population. However, when we are dealing with 'normal' or 'average' people, the effort of learning usually takes time: For studying, finding out facts, learning by repetition, struggling to understand, doing homework, and revising and testing. I will refer to this process, of learning by hard work, plus the time taken to learn, as 'taking up brain space'. So, brain space is really a factor of effort x time. Normal human beings only have enough 'brain space' to learn a certain amount.

Learning a language takes up brain space, as well as time on teaching timetables. If a school person is learning another language as part of their curriculum, they will need to attend lessons, and they will have to use their brain to learn lots of new words, vocabulary, as well as the grammatical machinations of that language. Most people find this process quite demanding.

Using the brain in different and challenging ways can 'exercise' the brain and be useful from that aspect, as well as teaching a person the art of learning. I do understand that. Nevertheless, learning a language does use up considerable brain space and teaching time, which is a finite resource. Let us look more closely at what that means in today's world.

Schoolchildren are faced with making learning choices, and quite early in their lives have to choose their options, or subjects, to learn and be included in their personal school timetable. They are obliged to study certain mandatory core subjects, such as practising their mother language and mathematics. In addition, they are faced with many other subject choices: Geography, history, literature, biology, chemistry, physics, art, design, computer studies, business, music, physical education, second languages … and other choices.

So, that is a menu of two core subjects plus at least 13+ other possible options (there are more). The normal child will usually reasonably cope with a total of 9–10 subjects in total during primary and secondary education, so the non-core options actually studied will be about 6–7 choices that they have to choose from the 13+ options. Therefore, choosing a second language has a lot of competition in winning a place in a school person's learning timetable and brain space.

Let us look at the choice of learning a second language more closely. Most schools offer a small variety of second language options from which to choose. So, which language should be chosen by the school person? Let us ask this question of a native-English-speaking person. With the exception of special interests (some prior knowledge or strong personal motivation to speak a particular second language) should your average English speaking student learn German, or French, or Spanish, or Chinese, or Italian, or Arabic?

The question often posed when making this choice is, which will be the most useful? Well, without a crystal ball to know a person's future career or work in this early stage of their life, deciding which language will be most useful to an individual is almost impossible to guess. One learns a second language to communicate in that language, but knowing which language is going to be the most useful is, for most people, impossible to predict.

So, the English speaking school person will normally choose a second language depending upon personal whim, parental preferences, or simple peer pressure (unless there are special circumstances). And, for many English-speaking persons, the motivation to spend their brain time on learning something that has no discernible advantage, and is quite difficult to learn, is low; and if they do choose a second language, frequently their motivation to learn becomes even lower over time when they start to wonder what is its use.

I have come to the conclusion that, for English speaking 'normal' children faced with this second language choice, I would advise not to opt for a second language. Why do I say this? Well, firstly, they have the very considerable advantage of already knowing the world's international language, English, and this huge advantage is rarely pointed out to them, unfortunately. And secondly, why use their limited brain space to learn something that may never be useful to them? Better to choose another, more practical option, and if it becomes necessary to learn a second language later in life when their motivation is much stronger, so be it.

In recent years, I have witnessed first-hand the second language option decision having to be made within my own wider family. I have kept quiet about the decisions, but what I have seen strengthens my belief in what I have said. Most young students, initially, seem to have some interest in this second language learning, but their interest very quickly fizzles out. It fizzles out because it is difficult to learn a second language, it is not used in their other subjects, and they find it hard to maintain motivation without any tangible advantage being obvious to them.

I realise a lot of language teachers will very strongly disagree with these observations, and talk about the benefits of broadening the mind and understanding another language. Apart from the self-interest of language teachers wanting students in their class, I doubt if they have thought about it from the student's point of view, and which second language to spend brain space on, and what are the practical advantages of learning that new language?

For several years, in the past decade, I have had to travel extensively on business around the world and within

Europe. There are very few European countries I did not visit during this work, plus countries of Africa, Asia, and the Middle East. I have learned a few basic words in some of the languages in the countries I have visited, for my own interest and politeness, and there is one language I can handle reasonably. But, I have to say, it has been rare, in fact non-existent, to have a communication problem on these travels as most of the time people who I have met or dealt with, both in depth or casually during travelling and eating, have understood English, or at least basic English, and given me understandable responses as necessary. So, the question does need to be asked – is it really worth using brain space to learn one, or two, or three, or more languages, in expectation of having to use them amongst the world's main 100 languages – when it is becoming increasingly unnecessary in this internationally English speaking world?

If this same question is now put to a non-English speaking person – which second language do you want to learn? – the answer is normally much easier. Learn English, as it is almost certainly going to be the most useful and practical language they can spend their time learning, and they can be almost certain it will be useful to them during their life, either for work or for leisure, or both (and it is easy to learn). That is why many non-English speaking countries now have English as part of their compulsory curriculum so the student may not even have to 'choose' English, as the choice is made for them. The motivation to learn English is all around them in movies, television, books, popular songs, adverts, usually parental encouragement and peer pressure, and they will understand and be reminded of the advantages to them for their future careers. Compared with their English speaking student counterparts facing the choice of which language to study, there is no contest; English is invariably the choice.

18. Is English Really Simple?

Without a doubt English is simple at the fundamental level of language learning, in comparison with other languages. This makes it comparatively easy to learn at the starter level and then to quickly achieve an intermediate level of competence: Using the basics of the language and being able to communicate reasonably effectively in familiar situations.

This simplicity is due to English not using gender or declension for its nouns and their associated adjectives, pronouns and determiners (declension means changing word endings depending upon use), and the very simple manner in which English regular verbs are conjugated (changing verb endings depending upon person, tense, voice, etc.). This makes English an easier language to learn at a basic level than all other languages which do have noun genders, declensions, and quite complicated verb endings. I state this, not only based on comparison with other languages and my own analysis, but also because many foreign English language students have told me English is easy to learn.

Most people that use English, but who are not native-English-speakers, spend most of their time using their English to speak, and to a much lesser extent, to read. Speaking is by far the most common way to use any foreign language, and speaking is quite forgiving in many ways. When you speak a foreign language, it is normally to another person, face to face, and by reading body language, and having a dialogue with another person, you can comprehend if the other person has understood you, or not, and you can repeat words, try alternative words, and alter your speed of delivery to deal with the situation.

There has been a lot of research carried out on the English language and it is generally accepted that you only need to know about 1000 words to understand 75% of basic English at the intermediate (middle) level. So, learning a language that is, grammatically, relatively simple, and being able to remember and use about 1000 words, is not that difficult. In addition, learners can hear English being spoken and sung almost constantly from a variety of sources, which enables such things as pronunciation to be practised and lodge in the memory.

The 1000 words, or so, in English remain the same most of the time, unlike many other languages that have declension. Noun endings change in many foreign languages, depending if you are simply referring to that object, or owning that object, or describing that object, or positioning that object, or using the noun as a subject or object; and it is important within those languages. We just don't do this in English, so once you have learnt the word, you use it without changing it, most of the time. This makes learning and usage of English so much easier.

Reading English is the other way that English is commonly used, and this is often used by scientists and other academics, administrators, and people within the commercial sectors that use English as their working language. People in such specialities quickly learn the

English words used within their specialism, whether it be in banking, the air travel industry, merchant shipping, medicine, etc., and then, in addition, they need to know fundamental English grammar and the approximately 1000 words previously mentioned. Reading is usually more demanding than basic speaking, but the advantage to reading in a foreign language is that sentences can be re-read until understood, and unknown words can be found in a dictionary, or Google Translate used.

Once a non-native-English-learner is using English regularly, they will quite quickly build up their vocabulary. Research has also shown that native-English-speakers use about 7000 words for 90% of everything they need to communicate. So, for the non-native-English-speaker using English, once they get to about 3–4000 words, they will be judged to be pretty competent at English.

It is true that English does have one of the largest bodies of words of all languages, called the vocabulary or corpus. There are about 170000 'root' words in the Oxford Dictionary, and this is a lot more than other European languages. However, this does not detract from the ease of learning at the fundamental level, and does have the advantage of giving English learners choice over specificity.

When English is used at more advanced levels, it does become more demanding, as do all languages. As well as being 'simple' at a fundamental level, English does have its own peculiarities, twists peculiar to English, and I will describe some of the peculiarities, below. Even so, these peculiarities do not detract from the fact that English is a simple language to learn and to speak, at a basic to intermediate level.

19. Peculiarities of English

All languages have peculiarities in grammar, punctuation and spelling. Below are described what I consider the main peculiarities of English that differentiate it from other languages.

1. Spelling and Pronunciation

In English, spelling, and consequently pronunciation, can be a bit of a minefield. In most Slavic languages, and in German and Italian, what you see is usually what you hear, with little or no variation. In other European languages, changes in letter-sound are usually denoted by an accent. Examples of accenting are 's' (as in send), or 'š' to change the sound to sh, as in shoe). The other European languages tend to be much more regulated, disciplined, and singular in pronunciation. English is much less disciplined, and is plural in its choice of pronunciation of its letters (I will explain what this means below).

There is the rather baffling use of many silent letters in English, which a lot of other languages do not use (for example, the 'b' in limb, the 'p' in pneumonia, the 'c' in luck, the 'w' in who).

There is the seemingly unnecessary and endless use of double letters (for example: letter not leter, tell not tel, full

159

not ful, rabble not rabel, pepper not peper) which are not used in many European languages, or certainly not as profligately.

There are diphthongs, which means two letters combined to form a different sound. For example, the diphthongs eu, oo, ea, ou, qu:

*eu*rope=urop   l*oo*k=luk   l*ea*rn=lern   *ea*rly=urly l*ou*d=lowd *qu*ad=kwad

And, there are very complicated letter combinations that seem to have no rhyme, reason, or logic at all:

through=thru enough=enuf colour=color coup=koo reign=rayn

In addition, there is no singularity in English of how most individual letters of the alphabet are pronounced. This can present quite a challenge to English learners. Starting at the beginning of the alphabet, 'a' can be hard, as in *atypical*; or soft as in *hard*; or either soft or hard as heard in different ways of pronouncing *bath*, or *path,* depending upon the regional dialect of the speaker.

'b' can be hard as in *broken*, or silent as in the ending of *bomb*.

'c' can sound like 'k' as in *can*, or like 's' as in *ice*.

'd' can be hard as in *dig*, or soft as in *riddle*.

'e' can be open as in *else*, hard as in *ear*, or silent as in *while*

'g' can be hard as in *get,* or soft as in *wage*, or silent as in *enough or tough*, and so it continues for most of the letters of the alphabet in English. The majority of European languages do not have this plurality of pronunciation of single letters with the consequent disconnect between spelling and pronunciation. There is usually only one way in which to pronounce letters and words in most languages, unless they have accents to change them. However, English does have this annoying pronunciation variation which cannot be deciphered simply by looking at the word.

A lot of this is unnecessary and should be sorted out (except English doesn't have a central language authority to do this). I do believe such spelling peculiarities will begin to diminish with the increased use of phonetic spelling as used in message texting. In fact, we are already witnessing this move to easier spelling, and it is very early days yet. I think the users of English, using texting and other social media, will start to change and simplify spelling, whether traditionalists like it or not. My own view is, bring it on and embrace the changes. After all, simplification has been happening for centuries, anyway; you just have to compare the spelling and spelling variations within Shakespeare, and other authors in centuries past, to see the constant changes in English spelling that have occurred.

Strangely enough, in my experience of teaching English to foreign students, this plurality of letter pronunciation is not the problem that might be anticipated. Certainly not in speaking, which is the main pillar of any language. Again, perhaps it is because the English language can be heard constantly in the environment that the pronunciation of 1000 words becomes well known. Spelling can be a problem in writing, but a problem about which most students seem unperturbed, or find interesting, or even amusing. At worst, mildly irritating. Even in writing, the reality is that spell-check is readily available to most people now, anyway.

The spelling and pronunciation aspect of English is possibly the main reason why some native English speakers believe, or want to believe, that English is a 'difficult' language. The success of the English language's global expansion belies this belief that English is difficult, and indeed, as I have previously described, the potential pronunciation problem is largely overcome by the ubiquity of English being constantly heard and available around the world. Undoubtedly, illogical spelling is a peculiarity of English, at present, but not the learning hurdle you might think.

2. Phrasal Verbs

A much stranger peculiarity to comprehend for the learner of English is our (ever increasing) use of phrasal verbs, probably a language phenomenon that most native-English-speakers are unaware of using, even though they constantly use them (as we don't teach grammar in our schools).

A phrasal verb uses a verb + preposition to create a meaning that is very different to its two component words (sometimes three component words). For instance, a common phrasal verb is 'take off'. 'Take' is the verb, 'off' the preposition. We use this phrasal verb quite a lot, and it has different meanings. An aeroplane takes off and leaves the ground. A comedian can take off a well-known politician by imitating them. A person can take off like a bat out of hell when they discover something requires urgent action. We take off our clothes to change.

Now, imagine you are a foreigner learning English. Yes, you have learnt the verb 'to take', and yes, you have a word in your own language that means exactly the same thing: to remove and hold. Easy. And, you understand the word 'off' as the opposite of 'on'. But how on earth, then, does 'take off' have so many illogical and different meanings: An aeroplane leaving the ground; or the skill of imitation; or to run away fast? There seems to be no logical link between the words and their meaning. It can be very confusing to an English learner.

Well, if that is confusing, what about the phrasal verbs: 'Take after' to mean resemble? Or 'take against' to mean dislike? Or 'take to' to mean like? Or, 'take up with' to mean to associate with someone? All using 'take' but with different prepositions. It is all a bit potentially mind-blowing.

In English, we have invented hundreds of phrasal verbs. There are presently about 200 in common usage, and about 1000 altogether. Very common phrasal verbs are: care for, take care of, pick up, ask out, add up to, back up, break down, call off, check out, dress up, fall out, get over...

These are all phrasal verbs that native-English-speakers use without a second thought. You can see the problem from an English learner's point of view; why on earth does 'get over' mean to 'recover'; or 'back up' mean to copy or support?

Phrasal verbs are on the increase, and it is an English language peculiarity (though I understand phrasal verbs are beginning to 'infect' other languages). The good news is that what appears to be a challenge for an English learner, in practice is dealt with by simply memorising them, and many English language learners even find their use interesting and amusing.

The odd thing about phrasal verbs is that whilst they appear to have no logic, in fact when used in context they seem to make sense, though it's difficult to explain why. Very 'English', some would say.

3. Inversion

English native speakers frequently invert their language, without realising they are doing it, and probably never think about it. So, what is inversion? Well, look at this conversation:

John: Hi, Mary. I'm going to the cinema tonight to see that new movie with Brad Pitt.

Mary: Gosh, what a coincidence – so am I!

The language inversion is 'so am I'. Do you see the inversion problem? Shouldn't she be saying 'I am also going', or 'I am too', both of which are readily understandable statements of intent. Instead, she is using what appears to be a question, or half question: '... so am I'. It almost demands a question mark. Does she mean 'so, am I going with you?' No, that isn't what she means; we know that. In fact she is speaking good, natural, English. She is making a statement that she is also going to the cinema, but unwittingly using inversion.

To a learner of English, this strange inversion appears to be a question, but without the questioning tone in the voice. However, questions usually require an answer. Instead of John speaking to Mary, let's assume Tomaz, a recent new learner of English, meets Mary:

Tomaz: Hi, Mary. I go to cinema tonight to see new Brad Pitt movie.

Mary: Gosh, what a coincidence – so am I.

Tomaz: Ah! Well, oh dear, hmmm, not sure … Do you want to go? With me?

Mary: I've just told you Tomaz, I'm going. I'm going with Susan, why do you ask?

See the problem? Tomaz thinks Mary has asked him a question '… so am I'. But, in fact, she hasn't asked a question at all but has made a statement, using inversion.

Inversion means the normal word order is 'inverted' (the opposite direction to normal). Inversion is advanced English, which native speakers use without thinking, and it is used for rhetorical effect, to balance the sentence, and does not have any grammatical reasoning. It's what we do in English, quite often, without thinking. Here are some other common inversions we use in everyday language (inversions in italics):

At no time *did he get* permission.

Not until the next morning *did she understand*.

Not only *did they arrive*, but they stayed.

Only later *did they learn* his secret.

Never before *have I seen* such bad weather.

You can plainly see there is plenty here to confuse poor Tomaz with this English inversion peculiarity. Fortunately, I'm sure he will learn to live with it, and probably over-use it with enthusiasm in the future.

4. Contractions

No, this is not to do with child-birth, but the English language. Language contractions are mainly peculiar to English, or certainly such wide use of contractions. English language speakers use contractions all the time, and they are increasing.

So, what are contractions? Contraction is reducing, or shortening, two or more words into one word, usually using apostrophes.

'It is' becomes it's

'Can not', becomes cannot, or can't

'Will not' becomes won't (bit strange that!)

'Should not' becomes shouldn't

'Would not' becomes wouldn't

'Could have' becomes could've

These are a few examples of contractions, but there are dozens more.

This, at first, can be confusing to English language learners. Most contractions are, in fact, used mainly in speaking, except the most common contractions which are increasingly acceptable in writing. For instance, the contraction 'it's' is now often used in writing, and so are 'can't', 'won't' and 'don't'. Mostly though, writers of English in books and newspapers avoid using the many other contractions that are commonly used in speech.

When an English learner has learnt to say "It is not in that direction", they can be a little confused, or even misled to hear "it isn't in that direction" (because the 'nt sound is quite soft, and can be difficult to hear for a foreigner). But, as it is also easier to say and remember these contractions, learners quickly catch on and begin to like the contracting process.

A bit more demanding for English learners, as they are unlikely to see these written, are contractions such as 'I couldn't', for 'could not', or 'I haven't', for 'have not'. However, they soon work them out, and using them once they have learnt the trick.

Becoming more demanding, though, are contractions such as 'I couldn't've', for 'could not have', and 'I will've', for 'will have'. It is contractions such as these that are not normally found in contemporary English language teaching books, and are highly unlikely to be taught by many English teachers that are not native-speaking-English teachers. In fact, I have even heard English language teachers deny that such contractions are correct. This is plainly untrue as most modern English conversations will contain many such contractions that are nowadays accepted. General use and acceptance makes them 'correct'.

Probably most difficult to master for English learners are contractions like 'I'd've thought', for 'I would have thought'. This use of 'I'd've' (or you'd've, or we'd've …), whilst being advanced English, can also be very useful, as the same abbreviation can be used for a range of words that the speaker does not then have to choose. For instance, 'I'd' can mean 'I had' (as in, I'd finished), or 'I would' (as in, I'd like). Therefore, learning and using this contraction technique can actually make speaking easier, once mastered.

So, most English language learners soon learn common contractions, if they are communicating with native speakers. I say 'if speaking with native speakers' because many 2nd language English users that communicate in English are not, in fact, usually communicating with native English speakers but with other 2nd language English users, and they are unlikely to be using as many contractions, if any. That said, the use of contractions is spreading to these 2nd language users also as it is easier to use them, once learnt.

So, I would place the use of contractions very firmly as a peculiarity rather than a difficulty, as they are not that difficult for English learners to overcome, are mainly confined to speaking, and once learnt can make speaking a bit easier and more natural.

5. The Possessive 's

Another English peculiarity is the use of 's at the end of words to show possession. For instance, 'it is John's bike', rather than 'it is the bike of John'. The possessive 's is used constantly in English, and it is one of the ways in which the language is simplified. Most other languages use the grammar model 'it is the bike of John'. This use of the possessive 's does not cause English learners a problem in reality, and they quickly learn how to use this simplification. There are some difficulties, such as it's versus its, and 's versus s' but, to be fair, these difficulties often wrong foot native English speakers as well as English learners.

It just makes you wonder why other languages don't use this very helpful trick of using apostrophes for possession and for contractions. Their unhelpful language regulators prevent this, perhaps?

6. Ed or T for the Past Tense

Having explained earlier in this book, courtesy of Abbot Cedric Pierre and his committee, that the past tense is formed by adding 'ed', such as 'I work' to 'I worked' or 'I play' to 'I played', there is the oddity of using 't' for the past tense, as in 'I learned' or 'I learnt'. When students become proficient enough to notice this, they can find it a bit confusing and ask if the 't' form is another verb tense. My short answer is 'no, it is not, and both are correct, but ed is by far the most common; don't worry about it.'

Using 't' for making the past tense is a much older form of English but has continued with some words, probably because it feels more comfortable. Some words must use the 't' form, such as 'built' and 'spent' because the 'ed' form of past tense for build and spend, i.e. builded or spended, do not exist and are clumsy in speech. So, in a few examples the 't' still rules the past tense.

Most regular verbs must use the 'ed' ending: climbed, smoked, washed, are examples. The words climbt, smokt, or washt do not exist in modern English (at the moment, but you never know).

Some verbs can take either ed or t. Examples are burned and burnt, leaped and leapt, spoiled and spoilt. There are about a dozen such popularly used verbs.

There is no real logic or linguistic explanation for these oddities, and though some linguists have attempted obscure explanations, they are not really convincing. There is a regional dimension to their different use. Americans do strongly favour the 'ed' form, whilst the British tend to favour the 't' form, if there is a choice, but this is changing with the ever increasing globalisation of English.

However, there are interesting small regional differences within Britain. For instance, in Yorkshire, England, the 't' form is much more favoured and here, unusually, you will often hear 'sempt' for the past tense of 'seem' (it sempt to me that he shouldn't have done that), whilst most of the country use 'seemed'. Sadly, I suspect, even such local differences will die out in the future.

So, these are the main peculiarities of the English language. Are such peculiarities a hindrance to learning English? Well the output, the number of English speakers in the world, would suggest not, and judging from my own experience, many of the peculiarities are embraced and seen as making the language easier or more fun, in some aspects.

20. British English and American English

Some English learners like to believe, and want to believe, that there is a significant difference between British English and American English. There is not.

I know of children being sent to Britain all the way from South American countries because their (very rich) parents want them to speak British English, not American English. Equally, I have heard students in Europe preferring to attend a language school that purports to teach 'American English' because it will be 'more use' to them in their careers.

The actual truth is that the differences between British English and American English are tiny in terms of vocabulary, grammar, and spelling. British and American people can always understand each other, easily. Except, perhaps, for extreme accents. A deep Southern American drawl may cause some British speakers a problem, but equally some pronounced English accents can cause Americans a problem (but they can also cause fellow Britons a problem at times!). The reality is, though, that the differences between the forms of British English and American English is tiny, and reducing.

Vocabulary. In terms of vocabulary, there are a couple of dozen or so commonly used words that are different between Americans and the British, and these are well known. For instance, the British say trousers, the Americans say pants. The British say hand-bag, the Americans say purse. The British say pavement, the Americans say sidewalk. Other examples are rubbish and trash, petrol and gasoline, boot and trunk, autumn and fall, cupboard and closet, nappy and diaper, flat and apartment, bottom and fanny, and tap and faucet. In reality, most British and Americans are well aware of these differences, mainly because of trans-Atlantic television and movies. There really is no 'big' difference between British English and American English vocabulary.

Grammar. Grammatically, there are very few differences. For instance, the British use the perfect tense (have + verb) more than the Americans. To give one example, the British say 'I have already eaten', and the Americans say 'I already ate'. Both uses, 'have eaten' and 'ate', are fully understandable. The British use 'got' for the past tense of 'to get', whereas the Americans use 'gotten'. Once again, both speakers fully understand each other. There is no 'big' difference between British English and American English grammar.

Spelling. Spelling differences between the British and the US in their respective use of English are equally few in number and quite unimportant, and even many of these differences are becoming blurred. The British use 'ou' and Americans use 'o', as in colour and color, labour and labor. Catalogue and catalog, programme and program, are further examples of spelling differences (though 'program' has certainly successfully invaded across the Atlantic). The 're' difference as in centre, center and litre, liter are other examples. Gray and grey are thought by some to be a difference, although both spellings are used by both countries at times. The Americans prefer sulfur to sulphur (and why not!), and they go traveling, whereas the British go travelling.

And then there is the vexing question of 's' and 'z', such as in realize and realise, and organise and organize. It is generally believed that 'z' is North American, and 's' British. That is presently true, by and large, but quick and easy research will quickly reveal that the 'z' form was once the spelling of preference in Britain. Such is the nature of fashion, even in spelling. What is interesting though, was how these small differences and fashions in spelling, vocabulary, grammar, and even pronunciation happened, and some of the myths surrounding the differences.

Color was actually used in British English long before 'colour' was used, and so was 'fall' (as in 'autumn').

The word 'gotten', for the past tense of 'got', was also old English (or should I say 'Olde English'?). And it was words like gotten, fall, and color that the Pilgrim Fathers took to the New World in the early 1600s. Meanwhile, back in Britain, we gradually changed to colour, autumn, and got; whilst the Americans did not. These differences were eventually 'formalised' by the first American dictionary-maker, Noah Webster, in the early 19th century, just at the time that the Americans were keen to differentiate themselves from their old colonial parent country, Britain, following their independence. Webster deliberately used the differences described, and also adapted the non-British 'er' instead of 're', as in center versus centre and theater versus theatre.

But, whether it be spelling, grammar, or vocabulary, the differences are very small and make no difference to the mutual understanding of both forms of English. Much to the disappointment of some wishful-thinkers and believers in the 'great difference'.

21. How Suitable Is English for the Modern Age in Which We Live

The basic prescriptive structure of a language provides the foundation upon which a language is built, and it is this basic structure of how to build simple sentences and communicate, that is called grammar. It provides a road map to set a person on the road of using a language competently. At this basic level, English is ingeniously simple, and I have described previously why that is so. It is this simplicity of the basic structures that makes English such a relatively easy language to learn.

I have also described some of the peculiarities of English, and how some of these peculiarities can prove a challenge to English learners as they advance their use of English (using phrasal verbs and inversion, for instance). I have also explained how some of these 'peculiarities' actually simplify the use of English (contractions, the possessive 's).

So, is English getting more complex, or simpler, or staying the same, as time progresses and its use spreads? I would say, without hesitation, that English is becoming simpler with time.

English is certainly not standing still. I have described how it is being used throughout the world with variations, and simplifications (pidgin English, for instance), how it is constantly adopting new words, and how the grammar is changing. So, it is certainly not standing still.

Is it getting more complex? I would argue strongly that not only is it getting less complex, but in fact becoming simpler in most ways. Yes, English is becoming 'larger' in terms of vocabulary, as are most recorded languages. Many new words reflect technological advances, along with cultural and social changes, but this happens all over the world with languages. Equally some words become defunct by lack of use. The Oxford English dictionary lists 615,000 words in 20 volumes and is easily the world's largest dictionary. But this simply means that the English speaker has a gold-mine of words from which to select, it does not mean the language is becoming more difficult.

But, how can I practically illustrate the language is becoming simpler?

I would take popular newspapers as a good indicator. First, let me deal with a personal incident. Many years ago, I bought an old house and decided to rip up the very old-fashioned lino in one of the rooms to replace it. Under the old lino I found copies of the local newspaper dating back to the 1930s (remarkable, really). Old newspapers used to be used as a form of under-lay for floor coverings back in those days. Reading this remarkably well preserved old newspaper was a real eye-opener. The text was 'dense' and detailed, using quite complex and verbose English, the sort of English to be still found in some government or legal papers, for instance. Yet, this local newspaper was aimed at the popular readership of its day, and what I was reading was obviously the standard of English that existed then. If such dense and detailed English was used today in popular newspapers, the newspaper would simply not be read and go out of business. This local paper obviously realised that fact, and adjusted and simplified its English over time, and is still in business, thankfully.

I am not saying that the average reader today is less well educated than they were in the 1930s. We simply live in an age in which our language has been simplified and will continue to be simplified. People today are certainly better informed about events that are happening around them, but the standard of English back in the 1930s was more complex, denser, and far less simple than the English used today.

What I have just described can be easily seen in modern newspapers that often publish, for readers' interest, what their newspapers were printing 100 years or 75 years ago. The British 'Daily Telegraph' does this regularly. A short read of these old news stories clearly demonstrates how the use of English has changed and is becoming simpler.

Admittedly, this only deals with written English, but it is a very good indicator of how English has been streamlined, and made simpler in speech also. However, we are now fortunate enough to have things like BBC archives going back to the 1930s, 40s, 50s, so we can hear the changes in spoken English. Listening to just a few of these BBC archives quickly demonstrates how ponderous, or verbose, or long-winded, or cut-glass – choose your own adjective – the spoken language was 60, 70, 80 years ago, compared with the present day. BBC programmes are now very much more relaxed, to the point, much more casual, and very often use regional accents, and sometimes even slang or vernacular. They reflect modern life which includes simpler, more relaxed, English.

Means of communication like Twitter, Instagram and texting are also having an effect. The demands of these methods of communication are making people use phonetic spelling and abbreviated grammar forms to get across their message to receivers. The use of these forms of communication are not limited to a few, and billions of messages are being exchanged daily by social media, and the effects of these abbreviated forms of English are trickling down into everyday English.

What I am definitely not saying is that this simplification has 'dumbed-down' English. Some people, especially traditionalists, will argue that English has indeed been dumbed down. I disagree strongly, and would suggest that we now live in a world where communication 'accessibility', for a much wider general population, has irreversibly occurred with the birth of social media, and is becoming increasingly important. English has the nimbleness, flexibility and adaptability to adjust to this need for simplicity and accessibility. Modern times, and the demands of modern communication play to the strengths of English, perfectly: its simplicity, flexibility, lack of regulation, and existing world-wide presence makes it the ideal language for this role.

Yes, English is becoming simpler as well as more relaxed.

22. Lack of Language Rules; A Good Thing or Not?

As explained previously, English is not regulated at all by any central authority, and accepted 'rules' for its use and its grammar are minimal. This enhances the power of English to adapt to changing circumstances, further develop, and accommodate the needs of users in different parts of the world.

But, this lack of rules does cause some problems for new learners, initially. New learners tend to like convenient rules, as it makes learning more disciplined. Many languages are firmly regulated, with plenty of 'rules', so many English language learners are used to having firm rules in their own language and are looking for similar rules to apply to learning English. They can be confused by the lack of such rules.

Here is one small example. Slavic languages have strict punctuation rules (which only apply in writing, obviously). These languages say commas must always be used before certain words, with no exceptions. We do not have such 'rules' in English, and we vary enormously in our punctuation formatting and have individual discretion, most of the time. Unfortunately, new learners do not particularly like individual discretion. They prefer firm guidance.

It is this freedom from rules that can make some English learners a bit uncomfortable at times, certainly new learners. Students like rules to make their learning easier and more disciplined, so English language teachers often pretend that there are more grammar rules for English than there actually are, in order to help beginner students feel more comfortable. It is when these students become more advanced that they are told that most rules are really advice or convention, many of which can be ignored.

This lack of regulation and rules is a very important contributor to the flexibility and growth of English, and gives it the freedom and space to flourish and develop. But, there are considerable numbers of English language specialists that would prefer to have grammar rules that have to be applied. I previously described the example of 'splitting the infinitive' (to boldly go), and the side-show of disagreement that went on between grammar theoreticians, and reality. To those grammar-lovers who think this flexible attitude to English grammar is just the demon work of modern lazy progressives, I also quoted the words of George Bernard Shaw, who could never be described as a 'modern lazy progressive' by any stretch of the imagination. He strongly objected to such grammar pedantry several decades before the 'Star Trek' programme with the ridiculous controversy over 'to boldly go'. Disagreement about grammar is nothing new.

This Star Trek example is not just much ado about nothing, but an illuminating glimpse into the type of tedious grammar battles that have rattled on within the world of English language for some years, between 'language lovers' (as they normally describe themselves) and practical users of the English language. These grammar lovers have probably not considered the bigger picture of English as a dynamic force, untrammelled by regulation and rules, with unlimited power to spread and adapt. They prefer to try and impose their own preferred rules upon the English language, and keep it exclusive. They invariably lose their battle, of course, and English continues merrily upon its path of further expansion and development, because it has the freedom to ignore such restrictions.

I do not dislike or reject 'grammar'. On the contrary, grammar can be an essential tool to help teach English to non-English-speakers, or even help native-English-speakers to understand English structure sometimes (as long as it is applied gently). I use grammar as a tool when teaching English, particularly for lower level students, but I repeatedly remind students that what really matters for their English learning and development is output, or practical usage of the language, not grammar theories. I remind them that an English language child of 3–4 years old can normally speak pretty good English and not have a clue what grammar even means.

Though I do accept and use grammar, I do firmly reject 'language lovers' trying to impose what they think should be a grammar rule, to be obeyed by others. If such language 'freezing' by the imposition of rules had occurred in the 17th century following the wonderful works of William Shakespeare, English would not have been able to further develop and blossom into the literature wonders of Austen or Dickens two hundred years later, or the beauty of Forster's books a further hundred years on. Shakespeare, Austen, Dickens, and Forster, were all using the English of their times. Their individual use of English prose was quite different, but each was understandable by modern English speakers, and each was beautiful in its application.

English is free and dynamic. This freedom from rules can be a challenge for some new learners, at first, but they soon learn to accept and relish this freedom. I only wish grammar-hugging native-English-speakers understood and relished this freedom with the same enthusiasm and reality.

23. Condensing the Issues Discussed in This Book

'Why the world is speaking English' is a deliberately contentious statement that contains assumptions that need addressing. Is the world really speaking English as the statement claims? What does 'the world' mean? How many people does it include, and how well do they use English? How does this use of English around the world compare with the use of other languages?

In this book I have tried to address these questions as well as explain 'why' this growth has happened, if this growth is increasing, and what might happen in the future. We have covered a lot of ground and dealt with many issues surrounding this astonishing growth of English, as well as discussing some questions concerning human behaviour and the use of languages for communication. Broadly, the subject chapters fall into seven categories: the history of the creation of English; the nature of the language; its size; the history of its growth; some peculiarities of English; what next for the language; and the potential advantages of using one language and disadvantages of using many languages.

Below is a summary of the key assertions in the book, but I leave the major question of: do we increasingly want to communicate more easily and readily between the different peoples of the world to increase understanding until the final chapter.

Here is a summary of the key assertions and facts in this book:

- Underpinning the astonishing growth in English is the communication revolution by which we can communicate and meet other inhabitants of the globe, electronically and by travel, and this has accelerated startlingly since about the year 2000. Like it or not, communication is becoming globalised.
- Originally, English had to be created to enable two separate peoples to communicate and live with each other. Thus, a simple, practical working language that could be easily assimilated quickly by the two communities, whilst being effective, was sorely needed. The need created English.
- English was a masterful melding of two very different languages, Anglo Saxon and Norman French, and was created to be simple so it could quickly be accepted.
- English is quite different to many languages in respect of knowing when languages began and how they were created. It existed by 1154, 88 years after the Normans arrived.
- English as we understand it today existed by 1154, and then a series of events ensured it was established. Chaucer and Wycliffe played a role in this establishment of English.

- English is not regulated, and this is one of its secret strengths. Consequently, the world can take what it wants, and give what it wants, to the language.
- It is a chameleon language, dynamic and forever changing, and roams around the world, absorbing new vocabulary
- Estimates of the number of competent English users are difficult to determine, but vary between 15% to 25% of the world's population. The proportion of the world's countries where English has some official status is between 41% to 48%.
- The emergence of Britain as a major world and colonial power, due to its dominance of the seas and thirst for trade, provided an excellent platform for the future growth of the English language. Interestingly, English grew within its colonies more by acceptance than force, probably because it was an easy language to learn.
- The continuing growth in English is due to many factors, not one silver bullet. The factors are many and include, in addition to its simplicity to learn, Hollywood, English language news, popular music, America, the Commonwealth, globalisation, advertising, the Internet, global commerce, English language education, tourism, and even T-shirts. All these factors work synergistically to enhance growth. The acceleration in growth in recent years has been due to the need for global communication, and the achievement of this possibility through technology.

- For the future, it might now be the case that we are approaching a time when there is a critical mass of English being spoken throughout the world, so people begin to feel vulnerable, or under-equipped, without this language skill, which makes it impossible to stop its growth.

- English is in an ideal position to become the international language of the world, and probably is already, as there is no competitor language with anything approaching the present advantages of English.

- Would the people of the European Union begin to feel more unified if they shared one language as happened in the USA? Would one international world language be able to greatly help bind the world community much closer together? These are highly provocative questions that almost dare not be voiced in this world where separate identities and cultures are highly respected.

- Perhaps it is time that such suggestions are more openly voiced and the idea of national cultures be questioned more? Indeed, in 2013, the President of Germany, Joachim Gauck, called for English to be made the language of the European Union because, he said, better communication and understanding is needed to build a more integrated European community.

- There are powerful obstacles against the concept of a world language. Language can be used politically and negatively to make communication and understanding more difficult. Language manipulation can be used, and is used, politically, for both positive and negative reasons.

- Using different languages does have a very significant cost which is barely ever mentioned. For instance, the EU probably now spends as much as €1.2 billion per year on cross language translations and interpretation.

- At a more personal level, is it really worth using brain space to learn one, or two, or more languages, in expectation of having to use them amongst the world's main 100 languages, when it is becoming increasingly unnecessary in this English speaking world?

- English is not only a simple language to learn and to speak, at a basic to intermediate level, but it is also getting simpler and more relaxed.

- English does have its peculiarities but do these peculiarities hinder the English learning? The number of English speakers in the world would suggest not, and many of the peculiarities are embraced and seen as making the language easier or more interesting.

- Differences between different forms of English, especially between US and UK English, are very small and make no difference to mutual understanding, though there are some wishful-thinkers and believers in the 'great difference'.

- The rapidly changing demands of modern communication play to the strengths of English almost perfectly as English provides simplicity, flexibility, lack of regulation, and an existing world-wide presence. This makes it the ideal language to deal with the explosion in world-wide communication and why it has outstripped potential competitors.

The next and final chapter brings together the facts, opinions, assertions and observations in discussing – do we increasingly want to communicate more easily and readily between the different peoples of the world to increase understanding?

24. Perhaps Not Really a Language Revolution, but Recovering from Babel?

This book poses the provocative question 'would it not be a better world if we all spoke the same language, and if so, wouldn't the obvious candidate be English?' A controversial suggestion, I realise, but one that at least needs to be aired in this increasingly connected and globalised world.

Whilst some may think that the proposition of an international world language, and I am clearly suggesting English, is a new and revolutionary idea, it is worth remembering that many thousands of years ago, according to Genesis of the Bible's Old Testament, humans did speak one language. It was when the people of this ancient world, following the end of the great flood, decided to build a Tower of Babel tall enough to reach heaven, that God punished them for being so disrespectful and He 'confounded their speech so that they could no longer understand each other and scattered them around the world using different tongues'. The site of this event became Babylon, then the largest city on earth, and Babel means confusion and is the derivation of the English word 'babble', or to speak meaningless words. Even if the Bible is not believed literally, it is still interesting that thousands of years ago different languages were seen as a creation to punish, not to provide cultural diversity. So, maybe the suggestion of having one world language is not that modern and revolutionary?

English is different to other languages in that it was created late in the history of human languages; it is very much a newcomer language, and it was created amazingly quickly. It was invented to fulfil a need, and was a necessary and practical creation to bridge the communication gap between two peoples, sharing the same island, with nowhere else to go and a practical need to communicate and integrate. It had to be simple to achieve this, and it is simple and unsophisticated in its basic form. This simplicity may be news to many people, especially those who like things to be difficult, but simple it is, and this is the first secret of success for English. Its simplicity.

English is also unregulated with very few rules. So, it has its own freedom to adapt and do whatever is practical for its users. This lack of regulation is very unusual amongst the other large languages of the world, and it is another of the secrets of success for English. It gives English a chameleon-like quality so that it can quickly adapt to new circumstances and regions.

English has also had a few pieces of luck to help it on its way (and all successes require some luck). The first was the establishment of the British Empire which was spread around the globe (upon which the sun never set), thus giving English a world-wide platform from which to grow.

The second piece of luck was that it became the chosen language of America, long before the potential power of this formidable nation was ever dreamt about.

Finally, it has benefitted from a magical combination of coinciding driving forces to propel the spread of English around the world, based from its rock-solid advantage of simplicity and adaptability. These driving forces are many, and include the allure of the American dream and culture, and its attractive products from Hollywood and Disney, the world-wide spread of English speaking pop music, the invention of the Internet and its English language prevalence, and the accelerating globalisation of trade and exchange of information.

This combination of simplicity, non-regulation, global spread, and the synergy of the different 'drivers' is creating almost a perfect combination to make English the international language of the world. It is in the right place, at the right time, with the right attributes, to be a principal agent to help with the change that is occurring the world over. A lot of people are concerned about this change within a globalised world, and globalisation does have disadvantages sometimes. Even so, globalisation and world inter-connectivity has many advantages. This world connectivity and exchange of information is not going to change.

It is true, to some extent, that change is nothing new to people of this world, but the speed of change does vary tremendously, and changes around the world are not equally distributed. In some places change at times can appear to be rapid, almost meteoric, whilst in other corners of the world, change is glacially slow. The speed of change can also cause a problem and provoke resistance, especially when it is fast.

Historians agree that life in general for most people, living in what is generally described as the western world, hardly changed between the medieval period to the 16–17th century, and then for most people it didn't change that much until the mid-18th century. In the lives of most people, important things like village and town life, travel, disposable income, disease, news, family values, clothing, housing and food, hardly changed at all, or only imperceptibly, for almost a millennium. Life, in short, for most people was pretty short, hard and grim. Yes, religions, politics, national boundaries, and rulers did change, often interspersed with frequent bloody battles and feuds that could seriously affect many lives, but life in general for the ordinary person did not really change that much for very long periods of history.

Now think about the last 100 years. Life for much of the world has changed very significantly. Around the time of the First World War, daily life for your average working family in western countries would still have been very hard work with few pleasures, travel for most was by foot, coal or wood fires supplied limited domestic heating, a very small range of food was available, simple diseases could lead to death, inequality between genders and races was legal and generally accepted, passive communication was limited to newspapers, if available, to a few, and letter writing was used for active communication. The 'world' for most people was really very small.

Much of that has changed dramatically for most working families during the time since that terrible First World War. And this time period is very short in the long history of humankind. So, humankind has had to deal with a lot of change over a short period of time, even though much of that change has been for the good of the majority of the population.

The most dramatic and highly noticeable change has been, by far, in communication and transport. Even 70 years ago (within the lifetimes of our parents), most people did not have telephones or televisions. Handwritten letters were still the norm for communicating. Travel, for things like holidays, was still very local, in your own country or even own county (if you had a holiday at all). Newspapers were more common and the cinema had arrived, but most communication 'news' was primarily about what was happening in your neighbourhood, region, or country. Most goods were made in your own country, and foreign goods were generally considered 'exotic'.

The revolution in communications and travel has been dramatic during the last half century. Now, most people have many different ways to communicate, whether it be by land-line telephone, by mobile, by the internet, tweeting or emailing, skyping or face-timing, and there seems to be other methods of mass communication invented almost continuously. What is happening all over the world is constantly revealed to us. We often know more about a war in the Middle East than what is happening in our own town council. Most people can travel to countries that our parents, and certainly grandparents, could only dream about, at prices affordable to the majority of the population. If we watch television news we will see interviews of people about a wide variety of topics, from all around the globe, live.

When I was a young man, much of the world was a closed society. China, the Soviet Union, considerable parts of Asia and Africa, were either closed to outsiders, or restricted, or places that, at best, we could only read about in more erudite journals or newspapers. Now, it is common to hear, and see, reports from Beijing, Moscow, Mumbai, Kinshasa, Timbuktu, Hanoi, and so on. Most places on the planet can enter our lives on almost a daily basis. And, when you see these people in faraway places, it is very common to see them wearing the same type of clothes as we do, driving the same type of cars as we drive, advert posters very similar to ours can be seen in the background, and the people on the streets are using their mobile phones.

This is the globalisation that is a reality. What I don't mean by globalisation are the highly contentious issues of shifting the production of goods around the world (though that is happening on a huge scale), or perceived scheming by international corporations to avoid tax and pay low wages, illegal laundering of money, or mass immigration, legal and illegal; all aspects of 'globalisation' that invite dislike and give it a bad name. The globalisation to which I refer is the undeniable and irreversible globalisation of communication, travel, and information about what other people around the world are doing. This is not going to change, and judging from the past 30 years will almost certainly continue to accelerate for some time yet.

I am sceptical of expressions like 'the global village', but equally we do now have a fairly good idea of how people are living in most parts of the world, and we seem to have an insatiable desire to know more. Long gone are the days when people in north England purportedly hanged a monkey because they thought it was a Frenchman. This insatiable desire to know more about the world we live in is not 'media led', as some conspiratorial theories like us to believe, but the media gives consumers what they want, and most people want to know what is happening elsewhere.

I am not saying this dominates our lives. It doesn't. We still have to pay our mortgage, earn our daily bread, look after our families, and be concerned about our health and well-being. But, we are also interested in what is happening around the world and increasing numbers want to travel to different countries. This is the globalisation of communications and travel.

The globalisation of production, and to some extent services, is also going to continue, despite the wish of some politicians to stop it and revert to trade protectionism (which is often a precursor to war, but that gets easily forgotten). The largest container ships can now carry up to 18,000 containers, and many thousands of these ships will continue to chug around the world transporting goods to and fro. They exist because we want goods from different parts of the world. We want lower prices and continually demand value for money. The matrix of business deals between the countries of the world will not cease. This transport and travel is now so cheap when done in volume, that fish can be caught in north Europe, be transported in refrigerated containers all the way to Asia where they are filleted and packaged, and then brought back to Europe for sales and consumption.

It is because of this relentless globalisation that there is an increasing need for a global language by which to communicate. All business deals require communication, negotiation, and organising. English is being increasingly used, not by imposition, but by market selection to fulfil this need.

Languages were originally created so people could communicate within their own group, tribe, or community, and almost exclusively 'internally' – with each other. Thousands of years ago, it was entirely reasonable to primarily communicate within your own group only, and this 'group' could be as small as an extended family, or tribe, in quite a small area. That is where life began, existed, and ended for the vast majority of people. Communication amongst one's own group was all that was important. This group-only communication is taken to the extremes in Papua New Guinea with their 800 separate languages, and they are good examples of how very local and 'closed' languages can be, and indeed were when first invented. It was all that was needed.

But globalisation now ensures that communication and negotiation is going to be increasingly outward looking with other communities. English was almost accidentally and ingeniously created to communicate between two different, opposing groups (Saxons and Normans), and it worked, so it has an old and proven track record of success and synthesising unity. The further example of the USA coming together as one nation shows just what a powerful tool a common language can be to get people to communicate and bond.

Communicating has to be a very good thing, and lack of communication a potentially dangerous thing. In addition to the convenience of the world's people being able to communicate with each other, a common language can also help people understand each other better, as demonstrated in the United States. Yes, to be united with

196

other people also requires other factors, such as similar social aims, aspirations, and values, but language is a powerful tool to help with this. When nations share a language, it does not threaten their identity or culture, as I have explained previously, it simply helps people to more readily understand each other, even if they don't agree on their politics, religion, or values.

It is very strange, is it not, that the governments of different countries often feel no compunction in trying to persuade, cajole, or even impose social systems upon each other, such as democracy, or capitalism, or religion, or socialism? Yet, when a common world language is suggested, it provokes cries of removing diversity, or culture, or identity from nations, when it can easily be shown to be untrue. Would some of the budgets of foreign departments of the USA, UK, Canada, and other English speaking countries not be well spent in encouraging and facilitating more learning of English, when it is abundantly clear from market forces that so many people in non-English-speaking countries want to learn this existing world language? I make no claim that it would solve the many problems that our planet faces, but at least it would enable the world's people to talk more easily about these problems and give them something in common; the gift of a common language.

I think this is going to happen anyway, and the journey to achieving this has not only started, but is well underway. I have no idea how long it will take for, say, 2/3 of the world to be able to communicate effectively in English, but if we examine the past, and how widely English has spread so far, it is obvious it is not impossible. There is also something called a 'critical mass effect' in wanting any knowledge, or goods, of any sort. When people are increasingly surrounded by other people that have certain goods, or knowledge, they invariably start to want it for themselves, and I feel confident this will happen, and is already beginning to happen, with English. The younger generation of many countries learn English much more than their parents and grandparents did. The way ahead is not to resist this desire to use an international language, and believe that using the same language as other people in the world is a negative thing; but much better to applaud this trend, encourage it, and welcome it.

Earlier in this book I explained that the invaluable gift to all humans was the gift of language with which to negotiate, to explain, to plan, to share, to communicate. Would the world be a better place if we could all more easily communicate and understand each other? I think so, like the Norman soldier and the Saxon peasant eventually did, 900 years ago. Perhaps it is the right time to overcome the punishment of speaking different tongues so we are unable to understand each other, as the Bible's Genesis claims happened?

Winston Churchill said many years ago, 'Jaw, Jaw, is better than War, War' (he used 'Jaw, Jaw' to mean speaking to each other). He knew better than most people a lot about the causes and terrible price of war between nations, so I think it would be circumspect to heed this advice. If we could 'Jaw, Jaw' in the same language, surely that could only be a wonderful aspiration?

Because of the driving force of necessity, English was created that is a language simple to learn, practical to use, adaptable to users, and flexible. It has been created by evolution (with a little help from Abbot Cedric and his committee), is readily available to all, and is well tried and tested. Let us encourage people to grasp this accidental but wonderful gift of English, and have even closer communication and understanding in this complex, and increasingly global world of ours.

END